1,309 DAYS LATER

How a dreary Lincolnshire market
town's hockey club went from the
bottom of a big pile to celebrating
league success

John Pennington

ISBN: 1469900386

ISBN-13: 9781469900384

This book is dedicated to the players, volunteers and committee members who have given their time to Grantham Hockey Club over the years.

CONTENTS

ACKNOWLEDGEMENTS

This has been quite a journey, both in terms of playing hockey and also researching, documenting and writing up a genuine story. It would certainly not have been possible without the assistance, generosity and encouragement of a number of people and organisations. This is by no means an exhaustive list and I apologise for any omissions made.

I would like to thank every player who has represented Grantham Hockey Club in their lifetime. You will have played your part in getting the club to where they are today. Other clubs to which I owe thanks are Grantham Town Football Club, who have been right behind us during both our difficult and good times and I congratulate them on their own promotion earlier this year. The very best of luck in the Evo-Stik Northern Premier League Premier Division. Lincoln Roses Hockey Club have also been supportive and Wellingborough Hockey Club helped me out with some fact checking. If you want to build a hockey club from scratch, those two wouldn't be bad examples to follow.

The Grantham Journal feature prominently in the book as before Twitter and Facebook they were the only means of publicising our results, news and reports. Sports Editor John Burgess has worked tirelessly to get our reports in the back pages, sometimes after I have unwittingly given him impossible deadlines. As a journalist myself, I should know better and your efforts have been much appreciated. His colleague Neil Graham was quickly on the phone to me after our 1,309-day wait was over and we were delighted with the back page coverage. He was also kind enough to run a piece on my other work which I was very proud of.

The staff at Grantham Library deserve a mention for allowing me to access the archives they hold there. To my friends who have offered me support and encouragement along the way by taking the time to read and download my previous work and give me feedback - all of which serves as motivation to keep writing - thank you ever so much. Some of you feature in the pages to come, some don't but in particular, I place on record my gratitude to Matthew Roebuck, Lee Hooper, Damien McLachlan, Fran Overbury, Peter Murray, Simon Higgs, David McDonald, Andy Nix, David Nix, Billy Tonner, Maria Ardley and David Haggart.

Thank you to Alex Clark for providing snippets of information and photos, some of which I have used in the book. Thank you to Sam MacAllister and Oli Phillips - as well as Clark - for standing in to write match reports when I was unavailable and therefore enable me to paint the full picture for you.

The Grantham Hockey Club committee, of which I remain a member, are also due some public praise and gratitude after the outstanding work they have done in keeping the club going during difficult times. Andy Nix and Andy Willey in particular have served outstandingly over a long period and David Sykes has done a sterling job in moving the club forward since replacing the author as chairman.

I must also thank my parents for instilling in me a love of sport and for ferrying me to matches and training sessions as a youngster. Thank you to the coaches and captains to whom I was charged when my hockey life began. They will know who they are but special thanks are owed to Brian Reed, without whom I would never have played club hockey as early as I did and Pauline Black, who recognised my ability to read the game and placed me accordingly in the middle of defence.

My ever-understanding partner Christina deserves some sort of medal for all she has been through. She was, perhaps, lucky enough to only meet me after we had started to win but still came along, rain or shine, to photograph the team as we embarked on the closing stages of our journey.

PROLOGUE – JOURNEY'S BEGINNING

Cast your mind back to early 2006. Twitter hadn't been invented. Facebook registration was open only to university students and George W. Bush was midway through his second term as US President. The only channel with which Grantham Hockey Club had to report a 3-2 win for their Men's 1sts over Loughborough Town in the East Midlands Division 2 on 11th March was a report sent in to the local newspaper, the Grantham Journal.

They could hardly have guessed that it would be over three years before their next league victory. Between then and late 2009, several players would turn out for the men in red, considerably fewer men would find the back of the opposition's goal and between 2007 and our next league win, I was one of them.

1,309 days and 69 minutes later on 10th October 2009, Grantham, resplendent in bright red shirts cast against the rapidly setting sun, led 5-1 over league newcomers Long Buckby and were about to end their barren run. Goals from Adam Phillips, Chris Keogh and captain Simon Higgs in the first half were followed by some nervy moments as the visitors grabbed a goal back in the second half. However, the men in red fought back and warded off a potential comeback with Phillips completing his hat-trick.

Standing on the sideline, the journalist in me started thinking about how I might encapsulate this historic game. I wondered how many national papers might pick the story up. As chairman, this will make a nice starting point for my end-of-season speech, I thought. Before I got too carried away, the umpire's whistle blew for full time. Arms were raised and cheers went up. Suddenly, even to me, unable to walk, it didn't seem so cold. The sun now appeared as a disinterested, insignificant third party. There was a positive warm glow around the team as they converged on the side of the pitch.

Only two of them - captain Simon Higgs and forward David Nix - were there back in 2006 against Loughborough. Young midfielder Alex Clark hadn't even started playing hockey then. After a few words of congratulation, I hobbled off. This was their moment.

000

WHY GRANTHAM?

Grantham was once a bustling market town, famous for being the place where Isaac Newton studied and the town where Margaret Thatcher was born. The football club, which plays its home matches on a pitch which is a misguided clearance away from the hockey team, gave Northern Ireland's Martin O'Neill his first break in management. It is no longer a bustling market town. It is no longer bustling at all. Several shops have closed and the town is frequently gridlocked with heavy through traffic that strangles the very life out of the place.

Anybody who can afford it takes their money outside of the town, preferring to shop in Lincoln, Newark and Nottingham. Having moved to Lincolnshire in 2006, the most frequent question I am asked is along the lines of 'what are you doing here?' Trying to win a game of hockey could hardly have cut it as a satisfactory response.

The continued search became a source of frustration and embarrassment. I dreaded the casual questions at work on Monday morning about how we had done at the weekend. Football and rugby-playing friends couldn't understand how a team could be either so bad or so badly handicapped. Truth is, we weren't a bad team. We were handicapped by the Midlands league being the only one in the country that insists that first teams must play first teams. We were simply out of our depth but with nowhere to go. We had to wait for friendlies against the likes of Peterborough 6ths or West Bridgford 5ths to get a competitive game.

Against that backdrop, is it any wonder that so many players decided they'd had enough and moved on? Even Higgs was to go the same way. Having captained the side for three years and finding it increasingly difficult to raise a side, he informed me in late 2010 that he would be resigning with immediate effect. If ever a league was set up to make the big clubs bigger and punish smaller ones, then this was it.

Yet we plugged on. We took nine players to Kettering and had to start with eight as they refused to provide an umpire. Somehow, Henry Young scored a goal that shook them up. We took eight to Market Harborough, nine to Leicester University but fought doggedly before eventually succumbing. For us, our target at the start of the season was to avoid conceding 100 goals. We managed it on one occasion. We would look forward to matches against new teams that we thought might be at our level, only to produce limp performances and unexpectedly lose. We had a captain not turn up for an away game at Buxton. I saw our goalkeeper break his ankle right in front of me. I played in a collared shirt with one good leg to fill a gap. We put two friends of a fellow player off hockey for life by fielding them after turning up short of a full complement of players. Higgs crashed his car on the way to a match, resulting in me starting my Grantham career on the left wing.

This is the story of how Grantham went from bottom of the pile to making local headlines, (allegedly) appearing in the News of the World, and my small part in it.

000

WHY HOCKEY?

I first picked up a hockey stick with serious intent to play back in 1994. After my family had moved out of Minehead into the quiet village of West Quantoxhead, I decided to join hockey club, held at lunchtimes as the distance we were now away from Minehead precluded me from playing sport after school.

From there I progressed through playing for school to making my league debut for Minehead 4ths against ISCA at Exeter University in 1997. I was quickly to learn an important lesson. Don't walk across the back of the goal when your forwards are warming up. A shot from one of our forwards crashed into my thigh and left me on the floor. I recovered enough to come on as a substitute and my only meaningful contribution to a match played on a well-kept grass pitch (remember them?) was to pounce on a rebound. Faced with an open goal, I slotted home during an entertaining 3-3 draw. The match was marked by one of our players - Nick Turner - being manhandled to a degree that his shorts were ripped to pieces. I learnt another lesson. This was no game for the soft.

A couple of seasons of toil and learning the game in the 4ths saw me shifted out to the right wing, where I enjoyed some success in creating rather than scoring goals. My natural position had always been somewhere in the back line and occasionally in goal, however, and it wasn't long before I was given a chance to play in defence.

I remember turning up to a club day at the beginning of one season and eliciting some surprise at being the only youngster that senior players could ever remember wanting to play at the back. I guess I already knew my strengths and weaknesses.

From the 4ths, I was the second player in my year to earn a call-up to the 3rds and remember working hard during a 5-2 defeat to Exeter & Culm Vale Hornets in cold conditions. Former ECV Hornets player Simon Chambers would be our goalkeeper when, ten years later, Grantham would also score five goals in their landmark win.

It is remarkable how small the hockey family can be sometimes. I am one of a number of Warwick University graduates that ended up at Grantham, for example. To add a further example, when I was at Warwick, I occasionally turned out for Berkswell & Balsall Common and in 2011, they were relegated to Grantham's league. I ended up playing against players who I had played (and got drunk) with at university. Suffice to say we might have had more chance of a result had we got drunk ourselves such was the gulf in class between the two sides.

Minehead 3rds were disbanded before too long due to a lack of players at the club and I returned to the 4ths. But not for too long. I made my way through sheer hard work and bloody-mindedness to the 2nds where I played alongside good friends and classmates Charles Parham and David Costello. On occasion when Costello was charged with captaining the side but unable to get to the start of the match on time I had the privilege of revealing the team line-up and formation. I even got to lead the side into action once, down in Exmouth. I lost the toss yet somehow ceded both choice of ends and pushback. I have rarely captained a club team since and I have every intention of it staying that way.

My graduation to play for the 1sts coincided with my time at Richard Huish College. The two years at Huish gave me the opportunity to play alongside and against some fantastically talented players. Mark House and Alex Bath, captains in my first and second years, were midfielders who could seemingly do anything and I have fond memories of our trip to Millfield where we finished second in the 2001 British Colleges Sport National Championships. We were a good set of players who took great pleasure in embarrassing the 'posh' schools by generally beating them on their own patch. We didn't even have our own pitch and used to train at King's College just up the road.

They dished out a 3-0 thrashing one dark winter's evening that gave us a figuratively bloody nose and left me with two more literally bloodied knees but there were better results to follow. A 1-1 draw with Taunton School and a thumping 6-0 win over Queen's College were highlights as was a 2-1 win over Millfield 2nds early on in my first year. Predictably, they pulled out a load of junior internationals for a rematch a few weeks later but could still only turn us over 2-1.

One of the highlights of my week back then was getting the bus into Minehead on a Tuesday night to attend club training. I owe them a huge debt in giving me my first taste of league hockey. It was and is a well-run club and while there is a strong emphasis on playing good hockey, in my time there it was just as important to bring youngsters through and look after them as they made their way through the ranks.

My coaches back then were Mark Swallow and Chris Stoner. They were hard but fair. As a young lad I remember being at the same time intimidated by them but motivated to do well to earn their approval. One evening, one of the team decided to question their insistence that you did not play with the ball on the wrong side. "It's easier," he claimed. He was challenged to dribble past Stoner using his reverse stick. Firmly tackled, he was shown that while it might be easier, it wasn't effective and to this day, I try to pass on the same method. I might not be allowed to be as robust in today's politically-correct, get-sued-if-you-breathe-on-me society but that was proper coaching. The message stuck.

Rob Setchell at Huish was almost the complete opposite. He was very laid back but got us playing for him. He passed on a piece of advice that has stayed with me and is an excellent one if you have limited time with your players.

Prior to our trip to Millfield in 2001 he told us he would not be wasting any time doing fitness training and it was up to us to get fit for the tournament as he was going to use his time concentrate on our on-field issues. I put myself through a six-week training programme in my own time that saw me lose half a stone. I have never been fitter.

Not just because of how far he has since gone, the best player I played against in my youth was Simon Mantell. Playing for my school in Minehead, we travelled to an annual championship for local schools, and generally returned home having been given sound thrashings all round. As if to rub salt in our wounds, this season Millfield were in our group and were about 7-0 up in the second half when Mantell came on, scored a couple of goals and disappeared again.

I would like to claim that my skills at centre back had forced their coach to throw him on as a last-ditch resort to win the game but little could be further from the truth. We were completely outplayed. I was never to face as skilful a player until I faced Matt Marriott playing against Wellingborough and I couldn't contain him either.

Before that though, it was time to move to Warwick, where I enjoyed several matches, several beers and made many friends through playing hockey. I missed the initial selection day so ended up playing for the 4ths under the watchful eye of Doug Macklam and Martin Stevens - both of whom I would later face when Grantham went to Berkswell.

The pair fostered an incredible team spirit and our little group was almost a club within a club. Time and again we would disrupt drinking circles and road trips with choruses of our 'fourth team 'til I die' chant. This spirit gave us a good run in my first year and when I took over as captain for my second year, we were on a roll and qualified for the knockout stages of the BUSA league. I thoroughly enjoyed captaincy and the challenges it brought. I remember frantic phone calls of a Tuesday night to secure players, committee meetings that went on for hours after training and then opening a beer at 10am in the spring when we found out that Harper Adams had somehow drawn with Oxford Brookes to hand us our place at the top of the table.

Typical of my luck sometimes, we were drawn to play Loughborough. We took the lead from a short corner, something that neither team expected. Goalkeeper Dave Haggart was later named the man of the match after he kept shot after shot out of the goal as we emerged the clear moral victors from an 8-1 pounding.

I was in the unusual situation in my second year of captaining the 4ths on Wednesday but playing for the 1sts on Saturday. There had been some opposition to me taking over as 4th team captain as I was considered good enough to play at a higher level. I was, but I didn't consider myself good enough to play regularly for the 1sts so was happy to stay in our bubble. I did once play for the 2nds against Birmingham University in a woefully one-sided game.

They scored 10 seconds after we had pushed back. We were 3-0 down before I touched the ball. You get the picture. No, I was quite happy playing 4th team hockey and then holding down the right back slot for the 1sts at the weekend in the Midlands league. We had a reasonable season, I enjoyed visits to Kettering, Coventry and Chesterfield and come the end of the year that was it for me. For almost seven years.

1. TAKING THE PLUNGE - WINTER 2007

In 2006 I moved to Grantham but it was not until the year after that I decided to start playing again. I'd dabbled with cricket but struggled to make an impression for Welby Cricket Club due to a combination of a long absence from the game, poor eyesight and back problems.

To ease my back problems I used to swim regularly and one Tuesday evening in 2007 as I was walking into the Meres Leisure Centre I made up my mind to get in touch with the hockey club. As I walked into the reception I could hear the team training to my right and felt immediately drawn to getting back into the sport.

The following Sunday I bought a copy of the Journal and on reading the report from Grantham's 11-0 defeat to Ashby, noted that they had only managed to field 10 players. I realised that if nothing else I ought to be able to make up the numbers, so gave Simon Higgs a ring, as he had posted his number with the report.

I spoke with him, briefly detailing my playing history, and he invited me to come along to training that Tuesday. I ordered some basic kit which arrived in time and off I went. It went well, I enjoyed it and was told to turn up on Saturday ready for my debut. No chance of easing me back in gently and little time to think about what lay ahead. I wasn't sure if my back would cope but I also knew that the only way to find out was to get out there and play.

Which is exactly what I did, but not until an unfortunate turn of events prior to the match getting underway. As the pushback time got closer, there was no sign of Higgs and news eventually reached us that he had been involved in a minor car crash on his way to the game. Fortunately, no one was injured but it did mean he was not going to make the start. Vice-captain and goalkeeper Stuart Gutteridge took over and having not been at training, stuck me out on the left wing.

I thought my days of running the wing were over. Not so, although given how Derby University spent much of the game in our half, there were few opportunities for me to attack. My over-riding memory of that match is running back from the halfway line as we defended a series of short corners. Simon eventually showed up and shifted me to a more natural position in the back line although I was helpless to prevent us going down by six goals to nil.

It was quite a debut. While the result and performance were hardly what I might have wished for, it hardly came as a surprise. I didn't think the students we came up against played particularly well and thought that if this was the sort of level to be expected we would quite probably pinch a few points by the season's end. How naive I was.

Next up was my first away trip, down to Corby, who play in bright orange shirts. They would go on to earn promotion and it was easy to see why, although we were far from disgraced as we were beaten 6-0. They had a team full of skilful players and moved the ball far too quickly and accurately for us to get anywhere near them.

However, following a half-time bollocking from Gutteridge, we managed to prevent them from scoring in the second half. That was some achievement, and my first experience of Gutteridge's passion. I have been fortunate to play in front of some top-class goalkeepers, and he is one of them. Time and again he was responsible for at least keeping the score line respectable and until Chambers' arrival and the subsequent emergence of Will Leadenham, he was missed when he left the club at the end of this season.

He remains a friend of the club and was among the first to offer his congratulations when we finally won a league match. That though, was a long time in the future. For now, I had to deal with a centre-forward whose response to being continually frustrated in the second half was to aim an elbow into my ribs. Unfortunately, he chose the wrong side to attack.

Working in Sussex in 2006, while supervising a softball game, I was rugby tackled by a well-meaning friend. Falling to the ground, I fractured some ribs on the left of my chest. 'Elbows' as I christened my orange-shirted assailant, had instead aimed for the right of my rib cage. It was probably one of the few opportunities he missed all year.

Next up was the visit of Ashbourne, who would go on to win and join Corby in being promoted that year. Yet again, we were unable to raise a full team and although our ten men fought hard, we were outclassed, many of Ashbourne's goals coming from short corners. The first goal I witnessed being scored for Grantham was little more than a consolation from Higgs, who according to the report that Sam MacAllister submitted to the Journal, 'shamed' the visiting defence. I doubt they lost too much sleep over it, finishing the season six points clear of third-placed Leicester University.

Like a bad tennis player, we were making a habit of getting thumped 6-0, which was the score line when we visited Kettering. Kettering were a team I had played against at Warwick but had since fallen down a couple of leagues. I was absent for this match and despite Kettering's relative fall from grace, they had more than enough on us. By now, I was beginning to understand what it was like to play for Grantham. It was like coming against a Mohammad Ali, a Phil Taylor or a Michael Schumacher every week. The only question was how badly we would get beaten.

Leicester University just missed out on promotion but would go on to go up - on goal difference - the next year, meaning that in the meantime they could help themselves to 12 more points from us. A 9-2 win at The Meres at least saw us grab two goals for the first time with me in the team and early on, we gave them a serious fright, goals from Richard Lawson and David Nix putting us 2-1 up. However, it couldn't last and the students' proved lethal on the counter-attack, and ran away with the game in the second half as our heads dropped. The Journal ran with 'Men Lose Their Morale' as their headline.

Unlike at the top level of sport, where the general order of teams doesn't fluctuate too much between seasons, at our level, teams can improve or decline remarkably quickly. An influx of two or three players can make a huge difference, as too can young players heading off to university. This is a particular problem that hurts Grantham. In my time at the club I have seen players develop from raw players struggling to make an impact to regular first teamers. Nearly every time this happens, they head off to further their education, and seldom return.

Oli Phillips is a rare exception and in a nice homecoming story, takes over the captaincy of the first team for the 2012/13 season although the club will lose Alex Clark, and soon enough, goalkeeper Will Leadenham, who has developed into one of the best in the area for his age.

Rolls Royce would finish just three places above Grantham in the 2007/8 season but would undergo a transformation and achieve promotion by winning the league one year later. On 24th November, we were given a taste of things to come when well beaten 8-0 away from home. An increase in sales of Rolls Royce cars coincided with their hockey team being on the upsurge. Clearly these players were as good Monday to Friday as they were on Saturday. I would make the joke a year later that if they were Rolls Royces, then we were perhaps Mini Metros.

The closest we came to a victory that season came in our next game when were beaten 1-0 by Standard, a team who played in Coventry. This was another one I missed and some typically creative work from MacAllister tells us via the

Journal that 'a slight deflection put a Standard striker through...who fumbled the ball into the back of the net'. It was probably a lot sharper a strike than that, unlike Lloyd Morris-Fletcher's penalty stroke which was saved late on, and despite concerted pressure, we were unable to find an equaliser.

Our second defeat by one goal followed away at Buxton, who beat us 2-1. Buxton was one of our longest trips of the season as we travelled into the Peak District. On this occasion, we made life difficult for ourselves thanks to an Adam Phillips own goal although Gareth Morgan levelled the scores. Alas, Grantham's hopes of returning home with a precious point were foiled and to make matters worse, Morris-Fletcher was sin-binned late on.

We then hosted Wellingborough, a team that only entered a team in the league for the first time in 2003 but had made sure they would be here to stay. We missed several good chances while they took most of theirs and as we pushed forward in a vain bid to get back into the game, they exploited holes in our defence to claim a 5-0 win. Like Rolls Royce, they would go from strength to strength and after consecutive promotions, now sit comfortably in the East Midlands Premier.

1,309 DAYS LATER

2. TWISTED REALITY - SPRING 2008

Prior to our first league outing of 2008, we enjoyed a club game. With no goalkeepers available, we placed a kit bag in the middle of one goal and a dustbin in the middle of the other. It says much for our predicament, lack of confidence and skill in front of goal that they proved alarmingly effective. I reproduce the entire report from the Journal of 11th January:

> "Grantham put two new goalkeepers to the test in a mixed event at The Meres on Saturday. 17-year-old Barry Bagg made a sensational debut for the Whites, pulling off exceptional saves to keep his team ahead throughout the game.
> "Following his outstanding performance, man-of-the-match Bagg is now in line to play for the men's first string.
> "At the other end of the pitch ex-professional Derek Dabin gave tips and training advice to club members.
> "But he was powerless to do anything about when the Reds were caught napping in defence, as the Whites overpowered them with powerful attacking play."

Never let it be said that we lacked a sense of humour, and we jumped on any excuse to get some positive news, even it was entirely fabricated, into the local paper. A few years later when a Sunday League official wrote to complain as a final hadn't been covered by the Journal, I was tempted to get involved in a heated online debate. Remembering that we had in the past effectively taken up column inches with a story about our players taking coaching advice from a dustbin, I decided not to wade in.

Back to reality and we then lost another game by the odd goal, 2-1 to Derby Asterdale. I always enjoyed playing against Asterdale, a well-organised, hard-working team who played the game in the right spirit. I had some intense battles with their centre-forwards and we took plenty of heart from this game, where it took them 20 minutes to open the scoring. My effort obviously made an impression on MacAllister, who saw fit to include me in the match report, although in the same line described Gutteridge as a 'veteran' keeper - I forget if this went down well or not. Asterdale led 2-0 at half-time from a 'dubious' short corner before Ross Booth grabbed a goal back for us. Asterdale went on to finish fifth that season, fourth the season after and then third, missing out on promotion by just a point.

The Journal's headline for our next defeat was 'Men come under repeated attack'. Ashby handed us an 8-0 thrashing, once again our resolve being broken after we fought tooth and nail to keep them at bay for 10 minutes. They scored four more before the break and then added three more afterwards. Such was their dominance that no attacking play from Grantham was mentioned in MacAllister's match report.

We were set for a more regular occurrence for our next game, making the short trip to Derby University to receive a 6-0 beating. Once again, the students were the ones doing the teaching, although no team needed to be taught how to pick the ball out of their own goal more than we did.

We were often much stronger at home - as most teams in any sport are - and for our next game, we gave leaders Corby something of a fright before being beaten 4-2. Home games usually meant more players were available to us and we at least, in theory, would be able to turn up on time and give ourselves every chance of preparing for games. Unfortunately, it seldom happened and our warm-ups would consist of smacking the ball at the goal. This infuriated some members of the club - me included - and it would be some time until this, and other bad habits, were eliminated. Unsurprisingly, it produced better results.

We went behind in this game but hit back through midfielder Mark Gray's first goal for the club. Gray has patrolled the central midfield area of the park since before I joined the club and will probably still be doing it after I have left. Never one to shy away from a tackle, a contest, or a word or two in the ear of an umpire, Gray plays with the tenacity and drive of a man half his age. Under his captaincy, we started winning regularly three years later.

For now though, we tried to stay on level terms but were unable to do so, failing to clear our lines effectively and being punished. David Nix thought he had scored another equaliser but the goal was disallowed, Corby scored again to make it 3-1 and Nix did get his name on the score sheet to set up a finish. However, the league leaders and eventual champions held their nerve and put the game to bed with a fourth, although we had made them work bloody hard for their three points.

Up next was our trip to Ashbourne, made memorable for so many bad reasons. Ashbourne is famous for its Royal Shrovetide Football match where the entire town turns out to compete. At times during a 7-0 thrashing it felt like at least half of the town was dressed in red and bearing down on our goal. From a personal point of view, matters weren't helped by the fact that I had been up all night commentating on a New Zealand v England cricket match that was taking place on the other side of the world.

I was disorientated and exhausted and remember turning in a terrible performance. At least I had a half-decent excuse. Some of the team had decided to stop at McDonalds en route, and played like a team that had gorged itself on burgers and chips.

Gutteridge let us have both barrels at half-time, singling out those who had stopped for a mid-morning snack for particular attention. He was well within his rights as he produced a decent display himself, marred only when a clearance from himself cannoned straight into my shin. After defending a short corner and finding out quite quickly that I was unable to put any pressure on my leg, that signalled an early exit for myself, and I watched in some pain from the sidelines.

This was one of my more disappointing days as a Grantham player. I was as unhappy as Gutteridge with the performance and the conduct of some of our players. My sore leg would rule me out of our next game, a 4-0 loss at Kettering, although it at least gave me a chance to rest. In an email to my parents I wrote:

"Pouring water over me during hockey games to stay awake has been a usual remedy (for fatigue). The last three games have seen our keeper kick the ball into my knee, shin, and thumb so I'm quite bruised. Also nursing a probably broken little finger."

With me also nursing a tummy upset, we were short of a full team against Leicester University in our next match, playing a quarter of the match with nine players with captain Higgs a late arrival. We produced an heroic display to keep the students at bay for longer than we should have but they eventually opened the scoring and then added another via the unusual (and illegal) method of palming the ball into the goal.

We toiled manfully but had little more to give and the final score of 6-0 reflected Leicester's dominance. We had been camped in our half for most of the match and our best chance came in the final seconds. Typical of our luck, Gray's shot went just wide. With MacAllister absent, it was down to me to send in a report to the Journal, and I ended with some optimism, not that it made the back pages:

"Grantham's remaining three fixtures see them play the three sides directly above them in the table and strong performances in those games could see them lift themselves off of the bottom of the table and register their first points of the season."

It wasn't to be, although we came agonisingly close in two of our final three matches.

Our penultimate match saw us host Rolls Royce and suffered against a team that soaked up our initial pressure and hit us with devastating counter-attacks to put the game beyond us. We had the better of the early exchanges but had only a deflection by MacAllister going over the bar to show for our efforts.

David Nix did get on the score sheet with a successful penalty flick after Higgs was fouled by the visiting keeper but that was a mere consolation goal. Alongside the Journal's match report, headlined 'Men hit on the break', they also ran a piece titled 'Support for first team is at an all-time low'. In it, Nix was quoted as saying "Support is at an all-time low. There used to be around 100 people turning up every week to watch games on Saturdays. That's rarely seen now."

For the next game we travelled to Coventry to take on Standard, in what would be one of their final games in the league. They pulled out ahead of the 2008/9 season and I remember this game, not so much for the 3-2 defeat we suffered, but the fact that I was voted as man of the match for my efforts.

I certainly worked hard and can remember making several tackles and setting up attacks as we took the lead but were pegged back before half-time. A goal from a short corner had us behind but we equalised through Ben Gascoigne on debut only to be denied late on when Standard notched a winner. In one verbal exchange with their centre-forward he came at me citing the score although weakened his argument by getting it wrong.

Nevertheless, they held on and took the second of their two wins they would manage that season. They also drew with Buxton to take 7 points. Buxton, who completed our season by beating us 2-1 at home, finished third from bottom on 22 points, some 15 clear of Standard.

In losing all 22 of our matches, we conceded 121 goals and scored 11 for a goal difference of negative 121. But would next season be any different?

2007/8 SEASON IN REVIEW

EAST MIDLANDS DIVISION 2

Opponents	Home	Away
Ashbourne	Lost 7-1	Lost 7-0
Ashby	Lost 8-0	Lost 11-0
Buxton	Lost 2-1	Lost 2-1
Corby	Lost 4-2	Lost 5-0
Derby Asterdale	Lost 6-0	Lost 2-1
Derby University	Lost 6-0	Lost 6-0
Kettering	Lost 4-0	Lost 6-0
Leicester University	Lost 9-2	Lost 6-0
Rolls Royce	Lost 6-1	Lost 8-0
Standard	Lost 1-0	Lost 3-2
Wellingborough	Lost 5-0	Lost 6-0

League Table

Corby 53 points, Ashbourne 51, Leicester University 45, Ashby 39, Derby Asterdale 38, Wellingborough 37, Derby University 34, Kettering 27, Rolls Royce 24, Buxton 22, Standard 7, Grantham 0

Corby and Ashbourne earned promotion to East Midlands D1

1,309 DAYS LATER

3. NEW SEASON, NEW PROBLEMS - WINTER 2008

Sport is a funny old thing sometimes. After Stuart Gutteridge had decided to move on to Lincoln, it was inevitable that we would be drawn to play against them in the opening round of the Lincolnshire Club Championship.

We travelled to Lincoln on a foul day and the game ahead of ours was delayed to the heavy rain that had left part of the pitch saturated. With no regular specialist goalkeeper available to replace Gutteridge, Andy Barton was making his first start in goal as one of several 'keepers we tried over the season.

This was, without doubt, one of the most remarkable games of hockey I've ever played in. With our university students available to us, we had a strong team out and pushed Roses hard. They play their hockey in the Yorkshire Leagues and as we were affiliated to Leicestershire so our paths rarely crossed - this Lincolnshire tournament being the only chance in a competitive fixture. Others aside from Gutteridge have played for both clubs and there is a strong link between us.

This occasion proved no different, although the home side quickly took the lead, showing their class with some outstanding passing and some slick short corners. However, we were aided by our 12th man - the weather. As the heavens opened, their quick passing game was nullified and the levelling of the playing field renewed our confidence. It turned into an end-to-end encounter and the goals started to flow.

Well into the second half as the rain continued, the umpires called a halt to proceedings. As both sides waited for a fairly rudimentary mopping up operation to be completed I tried to claim the game on the Duckworth/Lewis method, given that at the time we had one more player on the pitch, a Roses player having been sin-binned, and had scored more goals in the second half.

We got back underway and eventually lost an entertaining and enjoyable game 7-4.

We were due to open our league campaign against Standard - the team we had come desperately close to beating late last season - but they were forced to withdraw from the league. Over the next few years, us, Atherstone Adders and others would also withdraw, for differing reasons.

It meant we would travel to Derby University for our opening fixture, in which David Nix completed an unusual hat-trick. The students boasted some skilled players, were well organised and quickly found themselves ahead. After Nix had a goal disallowed for slicing the ball into the net from a short corner (for those unaware, the first shot must hit the backboard, which is about knee height), he scored to make amends.

Derby put us under immense pressure and scored when a drag flick beat goalkeeper Steven Metheringham. I distinctly remember being struck on the chest while defending a flick on the line. Pretending not to be hurt, I confess to getting away with one as it should by rights have been a penalty flick awarded against me. In cricket, there is a huge debate about 'walking' and whether you help the umpire make a decision or believe them to be there to make the decisions.

In terms of hockey, I am firmly in the latter camp. I don't think I have ever admitted to kicking the ball or deflecting the ball off the pitch, certainly not in a league game. On the other hand, I can remember several occasions when umpires have given fouls against me when no foul was committed. One such instance came during a match at Long Sutton when I made a fair tackle on the halfway line but was blown up by the umpire.

Having been on the wrong end of everything all afternoon, I quietly accepted it and moved back only to hear Andy Nix (David's brother) offer the umpire an analysis of what he thought of the decision. Not in an aggressive or abusive way, but nevertheless, he was sin binned for his trouble. The rough goes with the smooth and decisions do generally even themselves out. I play hard, and I play to win. I make no apology for that.

Back in Derby, his brother David completed an eventful first half by flicking a penalty stroke against the post after Derby were penalised and he would complete a remarkable set of goal, disallowed goal, missed penalty and sin bin when he received a yellow card late on. Derby were also reduced to ten men during the second half as the midfield battle turned a little ugly and they closed out the game with another drag flick and a goal from close range.

This was to be their last season in the league and as a number of their players went to play for Derby Asterdale, we were left to lament the loss of another couple of competitive fixtures and pizzas in the student union afterwards.

Our first home game of the season was against Worksop, who made the short trip down the A1. However, we turned up with ten fit players ready to start and captain Higgs unavailable, so our prospects were grim. Some serious cajoling from Barton convinced two of his friends - Alex Hunn and Will Tse - who had come along to watch to pick up a stick and make up the numbers. It was 15 minutes before we conceded, holding out bravely before Barton in goal was unlucky to be beaten.

A quick break resulted in a second goal when Barton was lobbed - unlike in football where a goalkeeper's hands are his main assets, a hockey goalkeeper is often hampered when the ball goes in the air and at this level is seldom able to control the ball effectively even if they do get a touch.

Barton was still inexperienced at this stage, but learning quickly at the same time.

David Nix maintained his strong start to the season with another goal from a short corner as we cut the deficit and then put Worksop under severe pressure with Tim Mihill impressive up front and Barton making excellent saves at the back. In what was by now a familiar tale, however, we couldn't make our pressure tell, Worksop scored again and that was the end of that.

Next up was a trip to Leicester University, where we had performed so well before caving in a year before. It was a similar match this time around, but they played even better and were quickly well ahead and able to put the match beyond all doubt well before half-time. They spent the majority of the match camped in our half and despite us being at full strength, we were powerless.

Mihill got on the score sheet after Leicester enlivened things from their point of view by sending their defenders up front and asking their attackers to defend, allowing us to at least maintain a record of scoring at least once in each game. It was about all we could take from the game.

We would take much more seven days later after playing our part in a five-goal thriller at the Meres against promotion-chasing Derby Asterdale. They went 2-0 up before half-time after a goalmouth scramble and slack defending allowed them good chances but we were not done.

Higgs fired an unstoppable shot into the roof of the net to give us hope and both sides then went on the attack, making it quite a spectacle of end-to-end hockey. We had the bruises to show we had been in a battle after the game, Barton and Higgs putting themselves in the firing line but it was to no avail as Derby scored to make it 3-1. They were not allowed to simply cruise to victory as Jem Hill swept home a cross to keep them honest.

They would eventually finish in fourth place, fading towards the end of their season but this was comfortably our best performance of the season thus far. Barton in goal was quickly growing into a confident keeper and an excellent shot-stopper, we had the benefit of a relatively settled line up at the back and in central midfield while youngsters like Hayden Richards and Chris Keogh as well as the Scotney twins - Alex and Tom - were all coming into the side and performing well under difficult circumstances.

All of the players mentioned above - with the exception of Hill - have since moved on to university or other sports. As a club, we like to think we have done our bit for the development of certain university hockey clubs across the country.

Our home game against Kettering a week later ended in a 4-2 defeat to the home side but the score line, as is so often the case, doesn't tell the full story. We felt justifiably aggrieved at having to start the game with nine men as our home umpire had not been able to make it in time. Higgs took the whistle as Andy Nix jumped into his car to fetch the official and while that was going on, Kettering raced into a 2-0 lead, taking advantage of the chaos we had been thrown into; their second goal deflecting off me and past Barton.

Going into the game, we had scored more goals than Kettering had and both of us were hunting our first win. With Nix and Higgs back, we held our own against a team that we already had something of a rivalry with from well before my time. We quickly got on the score sheet with David Nix hammering home after being given too much time and space in the circle. Kettering struck again, reacting quickly when a short corner broke down to restore their two-goal lead but we were not finished yet.

A driving run from Higgs ended with him hitting the post but the rebound favoured Grantham and Mihill tucked it away to put the game back in the balance at half-time. There wasn't quite as much drama in the second half, both teams having perhaps guilty of having expended too much energy in the frenetic opening exchanges.

Nevertheless, both sides had chances to score again but for 25 minutes neither goalkeeper was beaten until it was, heartbreakingly for us, Kettering who scored the decisive goal. A shot from the top of the circle went in, and summing up at the time I wrote "on balance of play, the away side were just about good value for the three points but with 11 men Grantham were more than a match for Kettering as the 'score' was 2-2 once the umpiring situation had been sorted out."

It wouldn't be the last time we would have cause to rue our misfortune surrounding umpires against this team. I played against Kettering three years before moving to Grantham with Warwick University in the league above where Grantham were. For the record, they won 4-1 on a scorching hot late March afternoon, but since then they had fallen on harder times on the pitch, consistently placing in the middle reaches of the league - never threatening to get promoted, but similarly never getting sucked in to a basement battle.

I was unavailable for our next engagement, a trip to Ashby. The team returned having failed to get on the score sheet for the first time in the season, going down to a 9-0 defeat. MacAllister's match report painted a fascinating - and entirely false - picture of Ashby surviving constant Grantham attacks to nick the game, despite David Nix having his stick shattered in his hands, Higgs taking a ball to the eye, 'stumbling blindly' back on to the pitch and Keogh being 'severely wounded' when a clearance was lifted into his chest.

Nix also hit a post, MacAllister had a shot cleared by a 'mass of tangled, desperate defenders' but the best line in his report, not much of which would have made the Journal, was his description of how Nix was unable to deal with this distressing blow to his hand:

> "The match was halted for a brief while as the force of Nix's strike had shattered his stick leaving very dangerous splinters in his hand. Grantham were not ready at the re-start, and with Nix still shedding tears Ashby capitalised and popped 6 in before half time - 2 of which were penalty flicks."

It doesn't seem to matter whether we play Buxton at home or away, but it is always bitterly cold. Their ground is perched high up in the Peak District, ours in a flat area away from the Vale of Belvoir. Despite the chilliness, we fought hard on our return to The Meres, only going down 3-1 to a strong team.

Little had changed. We had plenty of possession and several chances but could not score more than one goal, which was excellently taken by Mihill. David Nix repeated his trick of earlier in the season when he smashed the ball into the top corner only for the goal to be disallowed as you aren't allowed to do that from a short corner.

Buxton, on the other end, were clinical in front of goal and where I had got away with one at Derby University earlier on in the season, this time when a flick hit my shoulder, the penalty was awarded, and scored. At 2-1 at the break, it was anybody's game, and we pushed desperately hard, but were unable to convert a series of short corners and eventually Buxton's centre-forward showed us how it should be done, completing his hat-trick.

A massively different game followed two weeks later when we were back in action against eventual champions Rolls Royce. We started strongly, as we so often do, but Rolls Royce absorbed our attacks and hit two goals to blunt our optimism. David Nix had a chance to pull one back but shot wide, and that was about as good as it got. Although there were further chances for us to score - none were taken.

"Rolls Royce threatened each time they attacked but Grantham still caused them problems with constant interchanging of positions although further shots from Nix, Tim Mihill and captain Simon Higgs either went wide or were well saved by the Rolls Royce goalkeeper.

"Grantham stopper Andy Barton was powerless to prevent the well-drilled away team adding goals almost at will but stepped in on occasion to prove that the home side were up for the fight."

Up for the fight we certainly were but up to the standard of competing with Rolls Royce we weren't. Mini Metros were more like it, as we went down by 11 goals to nil.

Our final game of the year was down at Wellingborough, where we travelled with ten men. Given the quality of their play it was some performance from us to only be defeated by five goals. We worked exceptionally hard and during a period when they had a player sin-binned, we arguably matched them blow for blow before their numerical advantage was restored. However, our inexperienced forward line got no change out of their defence and we ended 2008 as we had started it - still trying to reacquaint ourselves with a winning feeling.

4. THE END OF A BARREN SEASON - SPRING 2009

2009 brought cold weather and a trip to Leadenham to play Lincolnshire's newest club in a friendly. I had a poor game, being completely at fault for the second goal in a 2-0 defeat, with both goals scored by players who had turned out for Grantham in the past in Ross Booth and Ian Sanderson. Two years later we would travel to RAF Cranwell, play against a side with more former Grantham players involved, and claim an important league victory.

Before Leadenham was set up as a league team, those that lived there or close by, including the Metheringham brothers - goalkeepers Robert and Steven - as well as Ben Lane and Simon Chambers, had to travel to Grantham to play league hockey.

When Leadenham entered the East League for the 2010/11 season, we kept a very close eye on their results as we were beginning to seriously consider doing the same. They encouraged us to make the switch and it was pleasing to see genuine praise for us as we won promotion - at their expense - in our first season out of the Midlands League.

Prior to resuming our league campaign, we had a club game at The Meres where the firsts took on the seconds, MacAllister describing the game between "two of Lincolnshire's most successful hockey teams in a clash of Biblical proportions."

The result was a rather entertaining 5-5 draw. "The titanic struggle to determine the best Grantham team was left unsettled as the 2nds, captained by Paul Hollingworth, held their rivals to a 5-5 draw," he added.

The seconds had a mighty impressive team out that day. Gutteridge was not on duty for Roses so turned out in goal and Lloyd Morris-Fletcher, who would have walked into our midfield during the regular season, led the line, although I did a reasonable job in keeping him fairly quiet. Nearly every one of the second team players on that day would swiftly progress to first-team hockey and those that didn't had finished their careers at the top and were winding things down.

Goodness knows what we would have given for a 5-5 draw in the league and when Derby University came visiting one week later we were handed a 12-0 thrashing. Another selection crisis saw captain Higgs end up in goal and with our outfield capabilities also weakened, we were easy prey for the students.

We were also working with a new formation that required me to play higher up the pitch, although it took me a while to work that out and experienced defender David McDonald was making his debut for us. Nevertheless, we put in a good performance and could take positives from the game, despite having conceded 12 times. Our inability to move the ball up the pitch from our own 16-yard hits was especially galling at times but we improved as the game went on and as my report noted, we made more tackles and interceptions than we missed.

Higgs was the fourth 'keeper we had used that season and I shared the man-of-the-match award with the post and our tactics.

Next up was Worksop, who at this stage were level with us on points after they started the season with a deduction. Their goal difference was the only thing keeping them ahead of us until they beat us 6-1.

Already, the time we had gone between wins was beginning to become something of a behemoth, as each potential opportunity to end the wait fell by the wayside, and I wrote:

"Opportunity knocked, but it proved to be a false alarm. Grantham went into their game at Worksop genuinely hopeful of putting their winless streak behind them but instead returned home having been clinically dispatched 6-1. So long is it since Grantham won a game that no-one seems able to put an exact date on the last time three points were picked up. Furthermore, just under a third of the squad in this game weren't even at the club when it last happened and Grantham's only goal came from debutant Will Walker. It is already a contender for goal of the season after he found himself with some space in the circle and drilled home a reverse stick shot with aplomb."

By the time he scored on debut, Worksop were 4-0 up and although we did not - and still do not - enjoy playing on a pitch that we find desperately slow, we could have no complaints. A combination of an effective pressing game and our struggles to move the ball forward from the back ensured we got plenty of defensive work to do and Barton - back in goal again - was named the man of the match for an impressive series of saves.

With no sign of the gloom lifting, I offered a similarly pessimistic view of the next game, closing with:

"Before the match, Worksop were level on zero points with Grantham and next week sees league leaders Leicester University heading to the Meres - for Grantham, they are no sooner out of the frying pan, than into the fire. Water, water, everywhere, but none as yet to quench the thirst for victory that burns so deep."

In my opening season, we had developed a habit - like the world's worst tennis player of losing 6-0. Now we reverted to a similar habit, although against Leicester University, it was 6-1 so we were at least showing some moderate improvement.

In fact, we made the students work exceptionally hard for their three points, and it was not until well into the second half that they took a firm hold on the game. Barton made some good early saves before conceding the first goal. We missed a good chance, repelled several short corners until eventually they scored from the set piece, much to our chagrin.

Leicester scored again after half-time to make it 3-0 before Higgs scored a wonderful goal. Picking up a loose ball, I fed him on the halfway line, stood back and watched as he bamboozled the defence and scored a solo goal with a cool finish.

A penalty stroke made it four for the students, Barton excelled again by saving drag flicks although another penalty stroke was won and converted by the away side. This was the same team that when we went to them, losing 13-1, they had dominated the match to such an extent that they used it as a training exercise. This time the points were exceptionally well earned.

As they had been by Derby Asterdale a day earlier, the Leicester match having been rearranged due to snow. Although the score line (6-0) was familiar, it did flatter the home side, with four of their goals coming from short corners.

We might have taken the lead early on and taken control of the fixture but we fluffed our lines. Meanwhile at the other end of the pitch, we had an experienced defensive line of Andy Willey, McDonald and Graham Johnson behind myself. Each Derby goal was well taken and Willey was yellow carded late on for a professional foul as we suffered a morale-sapping defeat, Jem Hill and Keogh also suffering injuries. We failed to register so much as a short corner or a shot on target.

From a morale-sapping 6-0 loss to a remarkable game which ended in a 10-1 defeat but given that everything conspired against us, that was a noteworthy result against Kettering. This was the same team that we had been forced to start with nine men against at The Meres. For the trip to their ground, we left with nine men, started with eight, took the lead and finished with nine. You couldn't make this stuff up.

It didn't make for a happy trip in the first place in the knowledge that we were two men short before a whistle had been blown. When we arrived, only one umpire was present despite Higgs having been promised that they would supply both officials - as we had done at home. They were having none of that as game time arrived and their coach was not prepared to do what we felt would be the honourable thing and take over the whistle. It left Higgs - as they only qualified umpire in our ranks - with little option but to sacrifice himself and officiate.

When England's rugby team was reduced to 13 men against New Zealand in 2003, and facing a two-man deficit in the scrum, inspirational captain Martin Johnson and a team of world-class players drew on all of their experience and skill to keep the All Blacks at bay. Kettering also play in black but we had MacAllister thrust into the role of captain, only one player left on the pitch over 30 and one natural defender - yours truly, as well as a full 70 minutes ahead of us.

Starting with myself, Mark Gray and Hill at the back, we startled both ourselves and our opposition by scoring early to make the score 2-1. Henry Young's first goal for Grantham is one that will live long in the memory, not so much for the detail of the strike, but the sheer audacity of doing it with a three-man deficit. Kettering were not happy. Higgs was not happy with the foul language they were using to express their discontent.

Wave upon wave of Kettering attacks produced some goals, but just as many, if not more, wayward finishes, balls that sailed over the sidelines and tackles from the committed Grantham team. We found the whole thing rather amusing but considered ourselves fortunate that we weren't playing with eight against a more disciplined side, otherwise goal-scoring records might have fallen by the wayside. I suffered a nasty blow to the shin as well as a fractured finger and we were briefly down to seven men when Keogh fell awkwardly and left the pitch with a damaged thumb.

As Kettering were now several goals to the good, our captain was allowed to take his place on the field as their coach decided that he would, after all, umpire for the final 20 minutes. Higgs almost scored to cap an eventful day for him but there was to be no fairytale ending to this tale. We simply jumped in our cars and left immediately afterwards, getting home quickly enough to watch most of our second team game at The Meres. It did little for our collective mood to discover that not only had they been able to raise a full side, but they also had a substitute to call on.

I am generally a staunch advocate of staying behind after a match and enjoying a drink and a meal with the opposition as what goes on during the game must stay on the pitch. After all, we are all playing the game to enjoy ourselves, but on this occasion, we felt utterly exhausted and extremely unhappy with the way things had transpired. There are some teams that I miss playing now we have moved leagues but I'm afraid Kettering is not on that list.

The roles were reversed in our next match as we had 13 players to call on and opponents Ashby arrived at the Meres with 10 men. Stuart Gutteridge was making a one-off comeback appearance and Rob Epton made his first start in a while and their experience gave us a boost. Ashby took the lead and we missed a golden opportunity to equalise when Hill ballooned a penalty stroke high over the bar. It might have scored a point in hurling but we still haven't got round to organising a tour of Ireland.

A swift break after a Grantham attack had broken down ended with Ashby going 2-0 up and we promptly had another shot stopped on the line and were unable to convert a series of short corners. Afer half-time, Barton had to leave the field due to injury but I was able to come on in his place and try to shore things up along with Epton, James Kerr and McDonald. Our initial efforts proved to be in vain, however, as Ashby quickly made it 3-0.

We were playing some of the best hockey we had produced all season and deserved something out of the game. Digging deep, we threw everything at it and pulled a goal back through Hill after an initial shot from Higgs had been blocked. The deficit was down to one goal when Young made it two goals in two weeks and suddenly, we sensed the possibility of a real result. Ashby gave us good as they were getting and I had to twice clear short corners off the line while a recovered Barton made several interceptions. We almost grabbed an equaliser as MacAllister and Richards drove us forward but the match was settled when Ashby broke quickly and launched an attack which was clinically finished from the tightest of angles. We left the field disappointed with the loss, but heartened by our performance. We had, after all, drawn the second half against a decent team.

Our 8-1 loss to Buxton saw us pass a landmark. As we came off the pitch having been well beaten, and with a number of injuries to show for our troubles, it meant the wait for a win would pass the three-year mark. Nobody was celebrating.

Like the flick of a switch, we went from a team that held its own to one that seemed unable to compete. We struggled to adapt to Buxton's hard pitch, with deflections and bobbles flying past our sticks but that cannot be used as an excuse for what followed, when we conceded seven goals in the second half having held the score at 1-0 against us at half-time.

And that too with Hill (knee) and MacAllister (fractured finger) suffering painful knocks early on. Buxton's opening

45

goal came as a surprise, neither side having created much in the opening period. They doubled their lead after the break and that knocked the stuffing out of us. They ran in goal after goal as nothing went right for us. We didn't help ourselves with some poor decisions and certain players putting more effort into haranguing the umpires than attempting to score a goal.

Eventually David Nix did score, drilling home a short corner, but it came too late to be anything other than what is euphemistically termed in sport a 'consolation'. I can assure you, we were far from consoled when the ball went in, particularly as MacAllister would miss the next match with his damaged finger.

We had a week off which helped some of us recover before we ended the season by conceding 30 goals in two matches against two of the top three teams in the league. There is not much more demoralising than sending the ball back to the halfway line after a goal has been conceded knowing that you'll be doing it again in, on average, around five minutes.

We travelled to champions Rolls Royce - their handsome thrashing of us clinched them the title - and with MacAllister absent through injury and Higgs having to umpire, had Gutteridge back again, but pressed into service as a centre-forward. Gray captained the side but even with his experience, we were horrendously over-run, forwards Young and Tim Mihill having to deputise in central midfield.

Robert Metheringham in goal produced several outstanding saves but we were comprehensively outclassed all afternoon. Gutteridge managed to grab us a goal with a low shot, I ended up with a bruised forehead after the ball popped up following a challenge, and as frustration got the better of us, Gray finished the day in the sin bin. Rolls Royce needed no second invitation to take further advantage by adding more goals, nine of them coming in the second half.

JOHN PENNINGTON

And so we finished the season at home to Wellingborough, who needed to win the game by 27 goals, as it transpired, to go up alongside Rolls Royce. At times during the game, they might have fancied their chances but aided in part by a hailstorm, we at least performed no worse than we had the week previously.

My acerbic opening to the match report on our website read: "Grantham completed their league programme with a stunning display of resilience that prevented their opponents Wellingborough achieving second place in the table. However, this Pyrrhic victory came at the cost of losing the match 15-1 to complete a 100% unsuccessful league season."

It is fair to say I had not enjoyed the game. MacAllister and Hill were back but could do little against Wellingborough's quick passing, sharp movement and clinical finishing and they raced into a 4-0 lead before the hailstorm slowed their progress.

Barton then received a green card for swearing after we had conceded another goal and we got on the score sheet through Richards but wilted alarmingly in the second half, which had become something of a habit throughout the season. 11 more goals were added - two from the penalty spot - but in truth we were all glad to get the game over with. Wellingborough had run rings round us, we had been upset by umpiring decisions that went against us and wanted to forget about another disappointing season.

The gory details read as follows: played 18, lost 18, scoring 16 goals while conceding 137 for a goal difference of minus 121. All that came without a regular goalkeeper, captain Higgs missing matches and a number of injuries hampering us.

Believe it or not, we felt we were moving in the right direction. The performances against Ashby and Derby Asterdale had proved to us, like the games against Standard the season before, that we were perfectly capable of giving teams a run for their money and it was surely only a matter of time before we turned performances into points. As it turned out, we didn't have to wait that long at all.

2008/9 SEASON IN REVIEW

EAST MIDLANDS DIVISION 2

Opponents	Home	Away
Ashby	Lost 4-2	Lost 9-0
Buxton	Lost 3-1	Lost 8-1
Derby Asterdale	Lost 3-2	Lost 6-0
Derby University	Lost 12-0	Lost 4-1
Kettering	Lost 4-2	Lost 10-1
Leicester University	Lost 6-1	Lost 13-1
Rolls Royce	Lost 11-0	Lost 15-1
Wellingborough	Lost 15-1	Lost 5-0
Worksop	Lost 3-1	Lost 6-1

League Table

Rolls Royce 41 points, Leicester University 37, Wellingborough 37, Derby Asterdale 34, Derby University 30, Ashby 30, Buxton 24, Kettering 15, Worksop 4, Grantham 0

Rolls Royce and Leicester University earned promotion to East Midlands D1

1,309 DAYS LATER

5. PLEASURE AND PAIN – WINTER 2009

I have had problems with my knees for as long as I can remember. Even at first school they would lock up after assembly on a hard floor, long car journeys often left me hardly able to walk and I own more knee supports than pairs of shoes.

One such is an old skateboarding knee protector and wearing this at university earned me the nickname 'Robo-Knee'.

It wasn't until the end of the 2008/9 season that I began to think I was in real trouble with my right knee. I got through to the end of the season but it began to feel sticky - or as a colleague at work would describe, 'grounchy' and moving it freely was becoming painful.

I hoped it might go away and opted to continue training. This proved to be a mistake. At a pre-season session we were doing some pretty basic warm-up sprinting exercises when the pain increased. As we went into a warm-up match, I went into the first tackle and the change of direction did for me. It felt as if something had snapped inside my knee. Straightening the leg was impossible without feeling as if I was being stabbed and I knew straightaway I wouldn't be playing for a long time.

Grateful of a lift to hospital from my boss, I was eventually examined, a strain was diagnosed and I was given a tubigrip to wear to prevent any unusual movement. If it was merely a strain, it is the most painful strain I've ever had. I was dismayed with the treatment I was given as at the very least I expected to have been given a pair of crutches; putting any weight on my leg was almost impossible. There was to be no follow-up appointment and I was effectively told to get on my way.

I had been appointed chairman of the club for this season but would take on a non-playing role for the majority of the year. The first signs that this would be a different season came in our pre-season friendlies.

We unveiled three new signings for our game against West Bridgford. Midfielders Benjie Groom, Rob Manson and Patrick Cutmore found themselves with Grantham as their local club after recent moves.

Although Manson would not play for us again, Groom and Cutmore played a full part in this season and a hard-fought 4-3 victory gave us plenty of hope, goals coming from David Nix, Tim Mihill, Manson and Adam Phillips.

As I wrote at the time: "Although Grantham will lose the services of (Sam) MacAllister, Mihill, Henry Young and the Phillips brothers (Adam and Oli) as they head for university, the way in which Cutmore, Groom and Manson looked at home in the midfield, and for that matter, the goal-scoring return of Nix, has left the squad feeling confident as they prepare for next week's County Championship competition in Leicester and then the beginning of the league season on 3rd October.

"Factor in the experience between the sticks of (Simon) Chambers and chances are that this could be a very promising time indeed for the club. Two weeks to go until the league begins with a trip to Kettering, but today, three was the magic number."

To qualify for inclusion in the Midlands League structure, despite us being in Lincolnshire and closer to Nottinghamshire, we were affiliated to Leicestershire. This compelled us to attend the annual County Championships, where we almost always came up against teams playing in higher divisions.

This year was no exception, and we lost 3-0 to Leicester, 4-0 to Coalville, 4-0 to Loughborough Sharks and 2-0 to Loughborough Town. Captain Simon Higgs was missing several players so Alex Clark made his debut and Ben Lane was also included in an inexperienced squad.

At least we managed to raise a full squad of players for the first league game at Kettering. Young, who had put in a heroic performance in Kettering earlier in the year was unable to complete the game, suffering from cramp, and Kettering dominated, although Chambers in goal produced a number of fine saves before we were beaten 5-0.

Our first home game of the season would finally end our barren run. Long Buckby had entered the league for the first time and had opened their campaign by being thumped 16-0 by Derby Asterdale. While we were by no means complacent, we went into the match confident as even though we were losing games, we weren't losing by that sort of margin to the likes of Asterdale.

It took us a while to convert confidence into goals as Higgs and Chris Keogh had shots saved, our first short corner came to nothing and Higgs hit the post. Our young midfielders Cutmore and Clark were playing well, David Nix was unlucky not to open the scoring until our dominance of possession told.

Cutting in from the left wing, Adam Phillips drove into the circle and unleashed an unstoppable shot to give us a well-deserved lead. After Nix saw a short corner saved, Phillips added a second and Keogh then hit the post again.

This was fantastic to watch and an unusual spectacle. Never before since I had joined the club had we taken control of any game, and certainly not enjoyed so many shots on goal. And still it continued, Keogh sweeping home smartly from a pinpoint cross.

We were 3-0 up and it got even better when Higgs capped a typically industrious performance with a fourth goal. Such was Grantham's overwhelming control of the game that Chambers touched the ball just once and Long Buckby failed to register a shot on target in the first half.

That changed after the break as the away side battled to try to make a comeback. Pushing the defence hard, they grabbed a goal and given our record over the last few years, we were nervous. No lead would be safe until the final whistle had been blown.

However, as if the goal had jolted us back into action, we attacked with renewed purpose and after their goalkeeper made a fine triple save from a short corner, Phillips completed his hat-trick having been fed by Hayden Richards to effectively clinch the game.

There could have been more goals as the game edged towards its conclusion but with both teams tiring, shots flew wide and too close to the goalkeeper, and Grantham's defenders played their part in making a little bit of history.

I wrote at the time:

"Grantham's previous league win came back on 11th March 2006, when they beat Loughborough Sharks by three goals to two and in that season, they went on to beat Buxton home and away as well as drawing with Derby University - having now rediscovered the winning feeling, Grantham will be keen to press on and taste victory more often.

"With a young, developing side, it is at least highly unlikely that we will be waiting until April 2013 to report the next victory."

I opted to leave the players to celebrate their win as I had played no part in it, aside from managing to fill in the right forms to register Groom and Cutmore as new players and sending them off on time.

It was, nevertheless, a wonderful feeling to be part of a winning team. Given that I had not played any hockey between 2004 and moving to Grantham, my own wait for a league win stretched back even further than the team's.

The 11 players on duty that day were: Simon Chambers, Simon Higgs (captain), James Kerr, Ben Lane, Adam Phillips,

Andy Barton, Benjie Groom, Patrick Cutmore, Alex Clark, Hayden Richards and Chris Keogh

There was plenty of Facebook chatter following the game, the most memorable quote coming from Clark, who revealed that Grantham's previous league win came before he had even started playing the game.

Only Higgs and Nix played in that game, and ready for a piece to go to the Journal, Higgs had me come up with some quotes from him. I added the following to a press release that I sent to not only the Journal, but as many national and local newspapers that I could find:

> "I'm very pleased with the win, it was a strong performance from a a new group of players that is still in the process of gelling as a unit.
> "Having played back in 2006 when we won three times that season, I certainly didn't expect us to be waiting so long for another win, although we have beaten teams in friendlies and tournaments in the meantime. I certainly hope that I won't be waiting another three years for another league win."

(You can read the full press release which appeared on our website, in an amended form in the Journal and according to a couple of players, the News Of The World, in the appendix.)

I received a phone call from Neil Graham at the Journal a couple of days after sending the report and he asked a few more questions and we were delighted to see that we made the back page of that week's edition.

A large photo of the squad sat below the headline 'VICTORY - AT LAST' and my own quotes were highlighted.

"I am extremely confident I won't be waiting another 1,309 days - which would be sometime in April 2013 - to talk about a win again."

I got that right.

We would, however, have to wait a little while for our next win and we were brought down to earth with a bump in our next game as we were beaten 7-2 at home by Worksop.

For periods of the game, we matched them blow for blow and a couple of goals from Keogh made the score 4-2 and the game was in the balance but the visitors were deserved victors, adding three more goals for good measure.

Watching on from the sidelines, I made a couple of observations in my match report:

"Playing fine hockey for 20 minutes might be enough to dispose of some teams, but not Worksop, who turned up with their game in good working order right from the first whistle and an array of short corner routines that carved through Grantham's defensive efforts....

"...both sides will be embarrassed about being called up for failing to apply the new five-metre rules correctly, and it was Worksop who were in the wrong on the majority of occasions. In the end, it didn't matter much, as they had the basics covered well enough to see off a spirited Grantham challenge."

The 2009/10 season was the first where experimental law changes were rolled out across all levels of hockey. No longer could the ball be hit directly into the circle from a free hit within five metres of the circle and the ball had to travel five metres before it could enter the scoring area.

Players were also able to take free hits to themselves - the self-hit. While the first innovation has introduced more creativity and increased safety for defenders, the latter has sped up the game and has met with almost universal approval, making it more fast-paced and interesting for spectators. It also means you have to keep your eye on the ball at all times and make sure you don't interfere with the attacking player taking the self-hit. It is rather like a quick tap penalty in rugby union and if used well, can quickly put your side back on the attack and take a couple of defenders out of the game.

Off to Ashby we went next and with the bare 11 players, were 3-0 down at half-time. A better effort in the second half, driven by midfielders Lloyd Morris-Fletcher and Benjie Groom resulted in a goal for Nix, but Ashby came back to score four more times on their way to a 7-1 win.

We then hosted Nottingham Trent University and were beaten 5-1. Parading a new set of shirts that I had worked hard to secure, we looked the part but our performance didn't match our appearance.

The students would not finish their league programme, withdrawing before we played them again and their results were expunged, leaving us a free weekend later on in the season.

We then travelled down to Wellingborough, who were already establishing themselves as the team to beat, having thumped Ashby 11-0 and Atherstone Adders 21-0 already.

We were handicapped again by being unable to play our strongest side, Higgs having to umpire which forced a reshuffle, moving Groom and David Nix into the midfield. We were unable to hold them.

Several short corners were won and then brilliantly converted as a range of slick moves, shots and drag flicks beat our men on the line and goalkeeper Chambers. We were further inconvenienced when Andy Barton had to leave the field with the ankle injury.

We improved slightly in the second half, keeping the ball more but getting no change out of a Wellingborough defence that would concede just 32 goals all year. We kept fighting but our opponents were too good.

We hoped we would be able to take something out of the following game against fellow strugglers Atherstone.

It was not to be as we were beaten 5-0 at home following a disappointing game in which we had never got a foothold. The early exchanges were fairly even but Atherstone made it 3-0 at half-time, the first coming via a deflection, the second a short corner and the third from open play.

Our woeful luck with injuries continued in the second half as we lost Jem Hill with a broken finger and although we were down to 10 men for the rest of the game, we kept Atherstone to just two further goals, which was a decent effort, at the very least.

I made my second team debut in a bizarre game at Daventry in the previous season where I had been hit in the head - accidentally, I hope - following a tackle and my request for a couple of seconds to compose myself was met with an order to go away by the umpire. We lost having taken the lead and I was left bemused.

Now I was an onlooker as we welcomed their first team to the Meres. They played outstandingly well, and despite a fine effort from Chambers in goal, led 7-0 at half-time to put the game beyond us.

We put them under some pressure as Higgs was taken out by the goalkeeper and David Nix missed a chance but we improved after the break.

Injuries to Hill, Cutmore and Barton left us short of options and when Richards had to leave early, there was nothing for it. Still wearing my collared shirt underneath a hastily commandeered red shirt, I entered the fray on the left wing with the score at 9-0.

With no shinpads, gloves or gumshield, there was no way I was going to do much more than try to keep it tight on the wing and I just about managed it, making a few tackles and some passes. It was good to be back, and most importantly of all, I suffered no reaction with the knee. Daventry scored before the end to finish with a 10-0 win.

Our longest trip of the year to Buxton was our next engagement. This must have coincided with occasional decisions to not bother sending anything to the Journal following some defeats. No report from this game survives, apart from to mention that we lost 5-0.

We finished the year with a 5-1 defeat at home to Derby Asterdale, at least ending a goal drought through a score from Keogh which made it 2-1 and gave us hope. It has become a sporting proverb of sorts and we can relate to it that it isn't the losing that kills you, it's the hope that does it instead. So many times had we got ourselves into good positions but this was another opportunity that wasn't taken.

Asterdale were 2-0 up when a quick break was swept home by Keogh but Asterdale's response was to simply score again and restore their two-goal lead. In fairness, they deserved to be clearly ahead as Chambers had again made several fine saves and the post had had its mettle tested.

Turning round at 3-1, we knew if we could somehow nick a goal, all hope would not be lost and we put in an excellent team effort to push Asterdale hard but their class told, adding two further brilliant goals to their tally.

Due to pre-season penalties and teams not showing up for matches, despite only winning one game, we were third from bottom at the midway point of the season. Long Buckby had claimed three points as Nottingham Trent Uni hadn't turned up but had an inferior goal difference and the students themselves were on -1 points.

1,309 DAYS LATER

6. BREAKING THE DROUGHT - SPRING 2010

We ushered in 2010 by hosting our old rivals Kettering, who beat us 4-1. I had declared myself fully fit to play and started for the first time all season. We conceded at the worst possible time, just prior to half-time which made it 2-0 to Kettering. From a game that was in the balance, the away side took control in the second half.

They made it 3-0 with a quick break after some Grantham pressure came to nothing, Will Walker and Clark unable to take chances offered. Kettering made it 4-0 after a defensive mix-up but we got on the score sheet when Hill, back from injury, smashed home a short corner with the last play of the game.

Now it was time for our trip to Long Buckby, one which we had targeted as a chance of claiming another victory. It proved to be an extremely memorable match and the 2-1 victory was my first league win for more than seven years.

It also saw Barton score his first goal for the club with the other goal coming from David Nix although we were hanging on at the end and Long Buckby missed a penalty which would have given them their first genuine result of the season.

It was they who started the stronger, attacking our goal but finding no way through our defence and wasting a couple of short corners. We gradually imposed ourselves on the game with Higgs and Groom in good form in the middle of the park and took the lead when Nix smashed the ball into the bottom corner.

Clark was having a fine game up front with Nix and he was named as man-of-the-match later on. 1-0 up at half-time, we were under no illusion that there was still plenty of work to do but it didn't take us longer than a few moments to double our lead, with Barton rounding off a fine move to break his duck.

Long Buckby were forced to trying to send long balls through us and reduced to the odd counter-attack but remained dangerous - it needs to be remembered that although we were in a winning position, we were not used to it, so were understandably nervy as the game went on.

They nicked the goal that made us even more nervous from a short corner, Chambers getting a touch but unable to keep it out. A frantic period of play then ensued and when Long Buckby won a penalty stroke, our hearts sank. Was victory going to elude us again?

Not so, as the stroke hit the frame of the goal and we then picked up our game once more, having further chances saved. There were a few more nervous moments as we tired but by the end, grim determination and a will to win got us home. I was exhausted having played more of a midfield role due to our dominance but delighted to be on the winning side for the first time in as long as I could remember.

It was one of the most enjoyable games we played that year. Although we had enjoyed the 5-1 win at home, it was something else to have been pushed hard and still come out on top of a closer game.

We took the same spirit and performance up to Worksop next time out where we were just beaten by two goals to one. Worksop, always boasting strong runners and skilful attackers, tested us far more than Buckby had and the early stages of the game saw us camped in our own half, but after they had a goal disallowed, we almost took the lead but Darren Hale's shot crept just wide.

Worksop then took the lead from a short corner as our back line was finally breached but at half-time it was 1-0, and anyone's game, mainly part to a wonderful performance in goal from Chambers, who repelled chance after chance.

Worksop made it 2-0 after the change of ends following a swift break, taking advantage of superior numbers after one of our attacks, led by Cutmore, Richards and Keogh, had broken down. We continued to fight hard, despite Groom and Hale suffering injuries, and got back in the game when Higgs finished off a smart move involving Walker, Nix and Keogh.

Now both sides pushed forward making for an exciting end to the game and both goalkeepers excelled in keeping the forwards out and I had to use all of my experience to marshal the defence and prevent Worksop from adding to their lead. In the end, however, neither team could score and both sides probably left the pitch reasonably satisfied. For Worksop, the three points were in the bag and for us, we had pushed them hard and continued to play as well as we had the week previously.

Into February and we hosted Ashby, a team who we had never previously got anywhere near beating. This time we were not only to lose, but had to say goodbye to one of our key players.

They took the lead from a quick break but we were playing some neat hockey, Walker and Keogh solid in midfield with Hill and McDonald strong at the back. We then failed to defend a short corner as the ball flew past Chambers as he charged out of goal. Down he went, and there he stayed.

It was clear something was not right and he immediately pointed to his foot, which was twisted in a way it just shouldn't be. He wasn't making a fuss but must have been in some pain. We were able to get some of his keeping kit off and make sure he kept still and warm until an ambulance crew arrived to further stabilise and treat him.

It was my job to phone his wife and inform her of what had happened. At the time, she had no way of getting to hospital and some thought was given to one of our substitutes driving Chambers' car out to her but eventually she did get to Grantham. Chambers made a full recovery from the dislocated ankle and went on to play for Leadenham, where he proved just as difficult a goalkeeper to beat as he was for us.

Hale took over in goal and did a fine job although neither he nor I could do anything about one goal as shot from a short corner caught a ridge in the pitch, flew past him, into my knee and into the goal. I wouldn't finish the match either thanks to that nasty blow.

Hale was also suffering an injury but he put that behind him to thwart Ashby on several occasions and for all their dominance, they could only score four goals in the second half to add to the three they had managed in the first period. A late attack earned us a short corner, which we missed. It was as close we had come to scoring but our thoughts were with our goalkeeper and his condition as much as any consolation goal.

Wellingborough arrived at Grantham the week after knowing that a win would seal them promotion and they duly delivered, beating us 7-2.

"...back to the recent past and Grantham actually drew the second half 2-2 at The Meres, home to not two, but three hockey goals these days, and a full set of lights, but shipping five goals in the first 35 minutes left them out of the match."

It was a poor first half from us and we had Higgs in goal for the second half Steven Metheringham having to leave due to work commitments. Higgs had produced one of the best goal-line clearances I have ever seen in the first half when, to borrow wording from cricket, he slashed hard and edged the ball onto the bar.

It was largely one-way traffic, however:

"...Wellingborough won a series of short corners but struggled to convert, line defenders Higgs and John Pennington making last-ditch saves, Higgs' the most spectacular as he upper-cut a shot onto the bar. So impressed was Pennington that he immediately conceded another short corner so Higgs might have another chance to impress the watching crowd.

"Eventually, however, the pressure told and once Wellingborough got their noses ahead, they grew in confidence and Grantham struggled to live with their fluid passing game, although they showed a profligacy in front of goal that prevented them from taking control of the game as early as they would have liked.

"Pennington thought he'd done enough to thwart another goal nearing half-time but the ball struck him on the arm and the resultant penalty flick was converted."

It was that man Matt Marriott who had returned to torment me one last time although I was convinced that on this occasion, the ball was heading wide.

We improved dramatically as the game went on, Keogh smashing in a goal to reduce the arrears to 5-1 and Clark also scoring when put in the clear. Higgs made save after save but the relentless pressure from Wellingborough was too much and two further goals were conceded, one scorching past Higgs into the top corner. Sometimes, you just have to accept you are second best. This was one of those days.

We were optimistic - perhaps too optimistic - ahead of our trip to Atherstone, who we genuinely felt we could beat given our recent performances and their position just above us in the league.

It was another false dawn, and a particularly disappointing one. It was a scrappy game with frequent heavy rain showers interrupting proceedings but that never usually bothers us too much. We had the opening chance through Clark but the home side took the lead when a shot across the goal just evaded Hale's dive.

They doubled their lead when a quick break combined with some sloppy defending gave Hale no chance from close range.

We felt crushed, upset with our own performance but we picked ourselves up, regrouped and pulled a goal back, Clark lifting the ball into the net after good work from his fellow attackers had lured the goalkeeper out of his goal.

Was a comeback on the cards? Not yet, although we had several chances before half-time to equalise, all missed as I got the sinking feeling that perhaps this wasn't going to be our day.

The second half saw us lose our hold on the game and Atherstone dominated, although to start with, shots on Hale's goal were few and far between. Excellent work from Hill and Walker got us close to scoring but Atherstone held firm, ready to apply the coup-de-grace.

It came from a short corner as the ball slipped between myself and Hale, with the predictable result of both of us blaming the other for its passage into the goal. Although our youngsters pushed hard to get back in the game, there was to be no way back this time. We were exceptionally disappointed with our performance as well as the result. We had not given our best and left knowing that had we played as we had done against Long Buckby or Worksop, we would never have lost the game.

The end of the season was beginning to feel like the end of any other season and the smiles from the Long Buckby results had rapidly faded away, and we still had promotion hopefuls Daventry and Derby Asterdale to come.

Only nine players made the trip to Daventry. I wasn't one of them but what must have been a sterling effort from the lads saw them lose 9-0 - a better result than when we had played them with 11 at home.

"Grantham knew it was going to be a difficult game ahead and the first choice was what formation to play with only eight outfield players and captain Simon Higgs chose a 2-4-2 formation hoping that the two players upfront would keep some of the Daventry players busy leaving the defence and midfield to deal with as few players as possible."

It worked well with no goals at either end for 15 minutes but as so often happens when you are a player short, we would inevitably have tired and Daventry created several chances.

It was 3-0 at half-time and six more goals were added in the second half and we just missed a late opportunity to notch a goal. It was surely no less than we deserved.

Our final home game of the season was against Buxton and despite myself and Henry Young returning to the side as well as Andy Nix joining brother David in the squad, it was a difficult day for us.

We did not make the best use of our resources and quickly found ourselves three goals behind at the break, a short corner bobbling into the goal, a goal swept in after a right-wing cross and a strike deflecting in off the post.

We were greeted by a heavy downpour of rain in the second half but it suited as and we enjoyed our best passage of play. Although we were able to win a number of short corners, we were unable to convert them and as the rain cleared, Buxton regained control of proceedings.

Steven Metheringham - back in goal now - made some excellent saves but was beaten one last time before the final whistle as we completed our home fixtures with something of a whimper.

By contrast, we gave Derby Asterdale another stiff challenge as we finished our league season away from home. On a gloriously hot day, the start of the game was delayed as some of their players hadn't turned up. Some players and captains might have denied them such leniency but not us.

Fortunately, when they were up to a full complement, we didn't embarrass ourselves, defending strongly and making breaks which caused them some problems. It was, however, a busy day for the defence and Higgs, who was in goal again.

With Sam MacAllister, Tim Mihill and Adam Phillips available, we had an industrious midfield to call on and on several occasions they combined to either break up or initiate attacks.

Such was our defensive effort that it took a goal of high class to open the scoring when a drag flick found the roof of the net. Higgs later saved a repeat attempt and both Ben Lane and I were on hand to make goal-line clearances as we frustrated the home side.

Our one short corner opportunity was blocked by a defender and eventually they killed the game off. When faced with two attackers, I was drawn to the man with the ball, who then slipped it to his free team-mate to shoot past Higgs.

"Grantham had few clear-cut chances afterwards; Asterdale had several, but a combination of good defending and wasteful finishing ensured that there were no further goals," I concluded in my match report.

It had been an eventful season, full of highs and lows. More lows than highs but compared to previous years, far more highs. The wins over Long Buckby were obvious highlights, but the way we played against the likes of Derby Asterdale and Worksop were especially pleasing.

Injuries had taken a huge toll on us, forcing important outfield players such as Higgs and Hale to deputise in goal after Chambers' unfortunate ankle injury. I believe that with Chambers in goal and the natural balance of our team restored we would have scored more than the six points we managed.

For the first season since I had joined the club we had achieved one other thing. We had successfully managed to concede less than 100 goals. 99 might be an unlucky score in cricket but for us, it was a nice number.

2009/10 SEASON IN REVIEW

EAST MIDLANDS DIVISION 2

Opponents	Home	Away
Ashby	Lost 7-0	Lost 7-1
Atherstone Adders	Lost 5-0	Lost 3-1
Buxton	Lost 4-0	Lost 5-0
Daventry	Lost 10-0	Lost 9-0
Derby Asterdale	Lost 5-1	Lost 2-0
Kettering	Lost 4-1	Lost 5-0
Long Buckby	Won 5-1	Won 2-1
Wellingborough	Lost 7-2	Lost 15-0
Worksop	Lost 7-2	Lost 2-1

League Table

Wellingborough 46 points, Daventry 40, Derby Asterdale 39, Worksop 32, Ashby 29, Buston 27, Kettering 26, Atherstone Adders 13, Grantham 6, Long Buckby 0

Wellingborough and Daventry earned promotion to East Midlands D1

7. THE HARDEST STRUGGLE - WINTER 2010

Ahead of the 2010/11 season we lost Sam MacAllister, Darren Hale and Tim Mihill, among others, to university and with Atherstone Adders and Nottingham Trent Uni having pulled out of the league, were expecting a hard season. That is certainly what we got, and there were more withdrawals and dramas to come.

There were signs of things to come when we could only raise eight players for a pre-season friendly with Spalding 2s. They were unwilling to lend us one of their subs for the day and we did a reasonable job in only going down 9-1. Of the eight players who played that day, Simon Chambers played outfield and Daniel Atkinson made his debut for us.

It was 0-0 at half-time but the extra numbers on a scorching day proved too much for us in the second half. We got on the score sheet when Gareth Morgan, who is now playing hockey in Belgium, scored late on.

For our next friendly against Peterborough, Benjie Groom, David Nix, Mihill, Dave McDonald and Chris Keogh were back having missed the Spalding encounter and it showed, as we produced some good hockey before eventually being beaten.

Goalkeeper Robert Metheringham was making his first appearance since breaking a leg in a car crash although there was little he could when a striker was put through on goal.

Peterborough went 2-0 up in the second half but had their goalkeeper to thank for keeping them in the game. We had several gilt-edged chances that were kept out and as we chased the game, inevitably gaps were left open, and another goal was added late on.

I was not involved in either of these two matches and had not been training for some time. I was struggling with a mystery stomach illness that was rendering me unable to eat, sometimes unable to move, and almost always feeling nauseous.

I lost a stone in weight, dropping to a point where trying to calculate my body mass index (BMI) on an online health website resulted in it failing to come up with a reading. I was hardly in a fit state to play but, as is so often the case with us, it wasn't long before I ended up back on the pitch.

Not for our first game though, against newcomers Market Harborough, whose slick passing and movement proved well beyond us and we were handed a heavy 11-1 defeat. For once we had a squad of 15 players thanks to the second-team game being cancelled but even had we used them all on the pitch at the same time we would still have been beaten.

It was 3-0 at half-time, our only chance falling to Will Walker, who hit Alex Clark - our own player - rather than testing the goalkeeper. Walker would make amends with a nicely taken strike in the second half but the game was gone by then, Harborough adding goals as they surged forward despite the best efforts of young Will Leadenham between the sticks.

Prior to a committee meeting after this game, Simon Higgs decided the time had come for him to stand down as captain. He informed me by email and then confirmed his decision at the meeting. I thanked him for the outstanding work he had done over the years that he had been captain, tirelessly raising teams which was proving to be more and more difficult. I didn't blame him for standing down but knew it left a huge hole to fill, and not just from an administrative point of view, as he was one of our best players, versatile enough to play in any position, equally adept at saving and scoring goals.

He continues to play just up the road from us at Newark having also represented Boston on occasion and still joins in at club events on and off the field.

We then travelled to Kettering and as I was absent, I had to try and formulate a match report from scraps:

"Following an opening week battering at the hands of Market Harborough at home, a match they lost 11-1, Grantham travelled to Kettering and performed significantly better before losing nevertheless 6-0.

"Chris Keogh marked his first game as captain with a committed performance but disappointingly picked up the first yellow card of the season late on.

"By all accounts, Grantham were somewhat unlucky to concede six goals and a couple of forays into the attacking third were unfortunately repelled."

Keogh's yellow card was particularly embarrassing as due to the fact that the rest of the team had left without him after he turned up late, his father had had to take him to the game, and therefore witnessed his son's transgression first hand.

I had noticed at the close of the previous season that Berkswell & Balsall Common, the team I played for briefly when at the University of Warwick, had been relegated the season before. Knowing who was in that team I quickly estimated that they would go straight back up - which they did, scoring 117 goals in the process.

I was always going to travel to Berkswell - or the University, the venue of their home games - and packed my kit just in case I was required. Still struggling with my illness, it took about five minutes before I was introduced.

Old team-mates Doug Macklam, Martin Stevens and Simon Tite were running the show against a young Grantham team in which Jack Fardell and Muzammil Pirwani made their league debuts. It was a tough baptism, and sadly one that I believe contributed to Fardell deciding that he would rather play football. Pirwani, on the other hand, kept at it, and enjoyed several strong run outs in the season after.

Atkinson suffered an injury early on and I was called on, enjoying battles with players I had teamed up with in the past but feeling frustrated with the helpless situation the team found themselves in. Despite Leadenham earning plaudits from the opposition for his shot-stopping, goals rained in - 23 of them.

Berkswell gained little from the match, and neither did we. While it was nice on a personal level to catch up with old friends, the match merely reinforced the problem with the league we were in. Berkswell's team were stuck in a different quagmire, too strong for this division, struggling in the one above. Like us, they had nowhere to go.

At this point I had marked the season down as one for development, of playing through the season, building experience and forming character before moving across to the East League, trying to ensure we continued to play the game in the right spirit and maintaining the social aspect of why we were playing.

Our second home game of the season was against Ashby. We 'dug deep and produced an inspirational performance', managing to draw the second half 2-2. Unfortunately, Ashby had raced into a 6-0 lead by half-time, but we were suitably proud of ourselves.

Keogh had managed to raise the bare 11, Ashby ran rings around us in the first period and although Leadenham had another cracking game, commanding his area and beating away shots, the away side turned round with a big lead.

On a rare foray forward in the second half, I managed what was probably my first ever shot on target in a Grantham shirt. The goalkeeper saved it but it went straight to Paul Hollingworth, who tucked away the rebound.

Soon after, Clark and Keogh initiated a clever break and Hollingworth added a second goal. Any chance of a remarkable comeback was swiftly curtailed with two Ashby goals but we had played the best 35 minutes of the season to date. For the first time, we felt like we were in a contest, rather than just being put up as cannon fodder for our opponents to practice attacking at will.

Leadenham was growing in confidence, Martin Halliday was also gaining vital experience and learning from it and Fardell had an excellent game, although sadly he was one that would get away.

It was back to the usual scenario when we travelled to Nuneaton - a man short - for our next match. I tried to lighten the mood before we got going by suggesting they had claimed an unfair advantage by putting green netting up around a building development next door - the same colour as their shirts.

Our defenders might have needed some hard hats too such was the ferocity and frequency of Nuneaton's attacks. We had handed a debut to goalkeeper Jonathan Watson and having not played for a while, I felt sorry for him as Nuneaton cut through time after time. Like Berkswell they had been relegated the season before but were clearly far too good for this division.

They scored 20; we barely threatened their goal. We did at least make it back to their clubhouse and it was interesting to note that they were going through a similar problem to us. A lack of players for them meant they had had to pull one team from the league. We plugged on with two teams despite not really having the number of players needed to put out two squads each weekend.

We were quizzed after the match by a player for one of the teams due on next about why we hadn't 'parked the bus'. That had never been an option for us and I was committed to turning up and trying to play.

What would have been the point? I can understand it if you are fighting against promotion rivals or need to get a result to stay up or stay in contention but that did not apply to us. It would become a more pressing issue in years to come but at this time, it would have simply impeded our development as a club.

With a full team at home to Long Buckby next, we fancied our chances of finally getting a result.

We started strongly, attacking from the off having welcomed back Tom and Alex Scotney as well as Mark Gray and we had early chances but were unable to take them. Long Buckby's counter-attacking style - rather like England's football team under Roy Hodgson - punished us for our profligacy when they converted a short corner.

We surged forward but found no reward and had to settle for 1-0 at half-time, although we sensed that if we just kept doing what we had been doing, we would eventually get the goals our play was deserving of.

The equaliser came when Tom Scotney swept home a right-wing cross, expertly placing the ball in the bottom right corner to leave the goalkeeper wrong-footed. We surged forward, so much so that I got into the opposition circle on occasion and eventually we got our noses in front through Clark, who nestled his shot in the corner having given too much space to shoot.

We held on relatively comfortably at the end to take what would be our final points in the Midlands league.

Just five players that played in this game had been involved in the win at Long Buckby in January and only three - Clark, Keogh and David Nix - had been playing when we ended the 1,309-day wait in 2009. It just went to show our inability to retain a settled squad of players. However, against Buckby, in any case, we had found our level.

It was an enjoyable game, played in an excellent spirit with very little niggle or hassling of the umpires but importantly for both sides - it was a contest. We had to work hard right until the final whistle to confirm our victory and they'd had to work hard to get ahead.

We were brought back to earth with a bump one week later when Worksop thumped us 13-0.

We were completely and utterly played off the park but kept our heads up, continued to work hard and never stopped running. Our attitude saw the umpires on the day both praise us after the match and email the club afterwards commending on us on our behaviour.

It was a rare positive.

For the home game a week later against Buxton, Higgs made a guest appearance for us and showed just how much we had missed him by scoring our only goal. Sadly, we lost the game 5-1.

A week later, it was time for us to give Derby Asterdale a good game and although they beat us 3-0, we once again made sure they had to work hard for it. So frustrated had I gotten by now with the way we were unable to raise a team, score goals or compete, I had even stopped sending reports into the Journal, hence the brevity of the details available as I describe a torrid final season as the whipping boys of league hockey in the Midlands.

1,309 DAYS LATER

8. END OF AN ERA - SPRING 2011

We opened 2011 with a trip to Market Harborough. The early start to the match meant a number of players were unable to make it and eventually we turned up with just eight players. To make things worse, we were late.

Chris Keogh and I were quite happy to concede the match before we started and let Market Harborough name their score and just play some sort of mixed friendly but they were understandably not so keen, so we braced ourselves for what was to come.

"The match, if it can be so called, was quickly over as Market Harborough struck quickly to take the lead although Grantham matched them for work-rate and determination throughout the match despite conceding goals regularly."

They are a good team. They weren't quite on the same level as Berkswell and Nuneaton, which was reflected in their finishing position of third, eight points behind Berkswell in second place.

They were plenty good enough to sweep our efforts aside as Will Leadenham, Graham Johnson, David McDonald, Daniel Atkinson and I were kept exceedingly busy at the back.

When you are under huge pressure and being pinned back game after game, you have to lower your expectations and aim for smaller goals:

"In the second half, with Grantham tiring and being found out of position, goals continued to rain for Market Harborough but Grantham took solace in managing to win a short corner and getting a couple of shots away."

I doubt I failed to take the opportunity to remind the Harborough team that they had a three-man advantage yet couldn't stop us getting into the circle. It really shouldn't happen.

We failed to take advantage of these brief excursions into attacking positions and were sent on our way having conceded 23 goals - at least we hadn't made a new record, equalling our goals against record for the season.

Hosting my not-so-favourite side Kettering was up next and they beat us 9-1, Paul Hollingworth scoring our goal as the goals continued to flow against us. I was away for the home match against Berkswell although we performed creditably to 'only' go down 11-0.

At this stage, a lot of us had had enough and were no longer really enjoying ourselves. Andy Willey and myself were doing much of the team selection and organisation ahead of matches and would inevitably spend most of Thursday and Friday evenings on the phone to each other trying to cover the latest setback.

For Ashby in our next game, it was no surprise that we travelled with ten players but something of a surprise that the majority of the team turned up very early and had time for a proper warm-up. Or we would have been, had our half of the pitch not been taken up by a junior session until seconds before the match was due to begin.

We were quickly down to nine men when Atkinson took a ball to the shin and opened up a nasty wound which immediately ruled him out of the match and the next one against Nuneaton:

"Grantham struggled to reorganise and soon found themselves fighting against the tide of concerted Ashby attacks and it wasn't long before they took the lead with firm shot from the top of the D.

80

"Goalkeeper Will Leadenham made a number of outstanding saves but even he had few answers to the Ashby attackers who burst through on several occasions.

"Some good work in the middle of the park from Chris Keogh and Mark Gray alleviated the pressure on occasion and wingers Alex Clark and Muzammil Pirwani showed good touches when Grantham broke into the Ashby half.
"One such break, right at the end of the first half, won a short corner, from which Clarke fed David Nix who smashed the ball home for a deserved goal."

Nix mixed brilliance with the agricultural and was sin-binned for a foul tackle late on and we found ourselves down to eight players - not for the first time in the season.

When he came back onto the pitch, we managed to get another goal, when Mark Gray drove strongly down the right and supplied a cross to Alex Clark, who swept the ball home.

12-2 was the final score and goalkeeper Leadenham was named our man of the match on another largely forgettable day for us all.

A short report was sent to the Journal for our next match, where we were soundly beaten by Nuneaton:

"Grantham were well beaten by promotion-chasing Nuneaton at the Meres while the second team proved a more difficult nut to crack for Ashby, who eventually ran out 3-0 winners."

How far we had slipped as the season went on was illustrated when we travelled to Long Buckby - against whom we had never lost - and were beaten. It wasn't even close as they despatched us with some aplomb by five goals to nil.

At least we managed to score against Worksop in our final home game of the season, Clark's finish being the highlight for us in an 11-1 defeat.

Our final two matches of the season - and of an era - would see us travel to Buxton and then Derby Asterdale - who we always seemed to end our seasons against.

The Buxton trip was a farce. With Keogh not at our meeting point on time, I called him several times and when I finally got through, could make no sense of what he was saying. With no clue as to where he was, and with us by now 30-40 minutes behind schedule, we had no option but to leave without him.

Several teams over the years in many sports will have left for matches having left players behind - or had players not turn up - but there can't be too many who have had to leave their captain behind.

It meant that I effectively captained the team on the day and we were soundly beaten:

"Goals against were inevitable as Buxton, who ended the season in fifth place, made clever use of their numerical advantage to engineer opportunities and although goalkeeper Will Leadenham was on top form, there was little he could do when outnumbered on several occasions."

We were further disadvantaged as Jem Hill suffered a nose bleed after being accidentally hit by an opponent's stick and he played no further part in the match having left an awful lot of blood on the pitch, the sidelines, and my camping chair that came in very handy.

Youngsters Tom and Alex Scotney, Will Hill and Clark performed admirably and we only conceded three goals in the second half and were happy to have won a single short corner and forced the goalkeeper into making a save. I was also named as our man of the match for my efforts.

And so it would be at Derby Asterdale that we ended our run of playing in the Midlands League. There was be no fairytale ending for us but we did at least get on the score sheet, the honour of scoring our final goal going to Clark. Asterdale won 3-1, they finished the league in seventh place and we quietly waved goodbye.

There was one table we finished on top of, however. After each match, the umpires rate the clubs involved on a scale of three to seven. At the end of year, these ratings were aggregated and our average score of 6.18 put us well ahead of everybody in the fair play rankings.

I was highly pleased with this as one of my stated aims when I took over as chairman was to engender an atmosphere in which we played the game with respect for our opponents and officials. After all, without the umpires you can't have a game at all.

The end of season brought with it mixed feelings. We were relieved to have got through it and got it out of the way ahead of a new start fielding one team in the East League. We had enjoyed some bright moments, with the win against Long Buckby and the improvement our young players - particularly Leadenham and Clark - were making was especially encouraging.

At the end of the season I decided to stand down as club chairman. Having at various points in the previous three seasons picked teams, run training, driven to and from matches, captained teams and dealt with issues off the pitch, I wanted to concentrate simply on playing - and reporting - when we began the next leg of our next journey.

2010/11 SEASON IN REVIEW

EAST MIDLANDS DIVISION 2

Opponents	Home	Away
Ashby	Lost 8-2	Lost 12-2
Berkswell & Balsall C.	Lost 11-0	Lost 23-0
Buxton	Lost 5-1	Lost 11-0
Derby Asterdale	Lost 3-0	Lost 3-1
Kettering	Lost 9-1	Lost 6-0
Long Buckby	Won 2-1	Lost 5-0
Market Harborough	Lost 11-1	Lost 23-0
Nuneaton	Lost 13-0	Lost 20-0
Worksop	Lost 11-1	Lost 13-0

League Table

Nuneaton 48, Berkswell & BC 47, Market Harborough 39, Worksop 34, Buxton 26, Ashby 22, Derby Asterdale 18, Kettering 13, Long Buckby 3, Grantham 3

Nuneaton and Berkswell & Balsall Common earned promotion to East Midlands D1

9. NEW BEGINNINGS - WINTER 2011

After the necessary administration was completed, we learned that we would begin life in the East League Division 6 North (North West) with a home game against Boston 2nds. We had played them in a friendly a couple of years back and despite at one point being down to nine men when Mark Gray was sin-binned, won 3-2 thanks largely to a virtuoso performance from Jack Hickmore.

Over the summer, we also had confirmation that we had been awarded Clubs First accreditation - an important landmark that we had worked incredibly hard behind the scenes to put in place. Without this accreditation, schools in Grantham would not be allowed to recommend us to any of their pupils showing an interest in the game, for example, and it means we have the proper processes in place such as codes of conduct.

Prior to our first league game we had a couple of friendlies lined up against West Bridgford and Worksop. The West Bridgford side gave us a stern test and despite myself, Andy Willey, Andy Nix and David McDonald working overtime at the back, they missed several opportunities to take the lead.

Instead, we got on the score sheet when David Nix finished off a short corner. Everybody got a bit of a run out in the second half and West Bridgford scored an equalising goal following a scramble and the spoils were shared.

When we took on Worksop shortly after, it wasn't the first team, who had been accustomed to beating us, that we faced, but a mix of first, second and third-teamers. Our 4-3 win - despite being reduced to nine players for a time - was especially encouraging and sent us into the first league game full of confidence.

The double sin bin came when Oli Phillips was given his marching orders for a robust tackle, the umpire showing no leniency despite the fact it was his first offence. Jem Hill's immediate analysis of the decision earned him a flash of the yellow card as well.

We had taken a 2-0 lead into half-time through Will Hill and Alex Clark, allowed Worksop to grab a goal after the break but a good left-wing move enabled Paul Hollingworth to put us 3-1 up when we lost two of our left-sided players.

We had to use plenty of nous and skill to keep them at bay despite a two-man advantage, employing rugby-style tactics of keeping the ball and then making sure when it left the field of play it was as far away from our goal as possible. It worked and when we were back to 11-a-side, David Nix put us 4-1 up.

Worksop then threw on a few first-team players with whom we were familiar and that enabled them to pull the score back to 4-3. We dug deep and for the first time since I started playing for us, the hard work was getting us rewards and more importantly, results.

But how would we get on against Boston? Pretty well, actually, and unusually, our short corners were outstanding. This made a pleasant change indeed:

"Grantham Men began life back in the East league with a 4-1 win over Boston 2nds, coming out on top in a game that was won and lost at the set-piece, with only one of the five goals scored coming from open play. Grantham scored three goals from six penalty corners won while Boston scored from their only such opportunity."

Boston struggled to keep up with us as we kept the passes short and the movement off the ball constant but their well-organised defence kept the game goalless. As we surged forward in numbers to try and get ahead, one of our best early chances fell to your author, whose reverse stick shot just crept wide.

Rob Buxton, who had fed me the ball, thought I had scored my first goal for 14 years, so close was it to going in, and he wasn't the only one.

A number of us were not happy with the way play was being allowed to continue after fouls were being committed and following a few comments too many, every one of us was given a green card.

We quietened down a bit and took the lead when David Nix's mishit short corner strike looped over the Boston goalkeeper and into the goal. It wasn't pretty, but no one could deny we deserved to be ahead.

There was a good reason why we were agitated at not being given fouls in the circle. We knew our short corners would give us a good chance of scoring and wanted as many opportunities as we could muster.

We made a poor start to the second half and Boston equalised after six minutes when from a short corner they drilled a shot between goalkeeper Will Leadenham and me on the post.

Four minutes later we were ahead again as Gray swept home from a short corner and although that settled us, we needed the benefit of Nick Wraith's experience at sweeper to bail us out on occasion.

Wraith, who has been a wonderful servant to the club over the years, keeps threatening to retire as each season comes round but we try our best to dissuade him. Vastly experienced, he is one of those players with an incredible ability to read the game and be in exactly the right place to make a telling tackle or pass.

Another short corner strike from Nix saw us pull two goals ahead and that was the blow that finally killed off Boston's hopes. We hit a post in the closing moments and made it 4-1 with seconds remaining through Hollingworth, who nutmegged the goalkeeper having been put through by Nix.

It was a satisfactory start to life in our new league but I felt the score line flattered us a touch as up until we scored late on, Boston could easily have snatched something from the game. Nobody was complaining as for the last few years, we had been on the other end of such matches, and lost games we might have otherwise won.

I missed the trip to Spalding, where we recovered from 2-1 down at half-time to win 6-3 on one of the hottest days of the year during an Indian summer. I dislike playing hockey in the sun, it being one of the reasons I try to avoid playing in the summer, so I wasn't too disappointed to have missed out. I would find out later on in the season that Spalding's recent pitch upgrade has not included showering facilities. It can't have been a comfortable drive back home.

We were down to ten men on three separate occasions during the game; having been rewarded for our good behaviour last season, we had now picked up 12 greens and two yellows in two matches. Clark and Gray were the men to see yellow and Wraith suffered an injury but we dug deep, scored some wonderful goals, Paul Hollingworth and Oli Phillips grabbing a brace and Clark scoring a 'sumptuous' drag flick.

Our unbeaten run came to an abrupt end soon after against Long Sutton 3rds. It was another warm day and it took a fine goal to separate the two teams, Long Sutton eventually converting one of a plethora of short corners with a drag flick.

They did have the ball in the goal in the first half and although I couldn't see anything wrong with the goal from my vantage point, it was chalked off for an earlier offence. It was a midfield battle and aside from the disallowed goal, Long Sutton rarely threatened our goal from open play. On one occasion, they had three men through on goal but failed to score. We were unable to take advantage, missing good chances ourselves and then paying the penalty.

As described in a previous chapter, Andy Nix was later sin binned for reacting to an umpire's decision to give Long Sutton a free hit after I made a clean tackle on the halfway line. I wasn't too bothered with the poor decision but was less than impressed with my team-mate's reaction. When he came back on the pitch I encouraged him to run a little quicker than he was as after all he'd had ten minutes to rest. My own brand of encouraging my team-mates wasn't quite enough, however, and we left disappointed as well as hot and bothered. There was at least a decent post-match meal waiting for us and I tweeted a picture of battered sausage and chips with the comment 'every post-match meal should be this good'.

We would have to wait to get back to league action, entertaining West Bridgford 5ths in a friendly at the Meres. For the second week running, we were beaten by the odd goal, our visitors returning with a 3-2 win in their kit bags.

We were again undone by short corners, conceding all three goals from the set piece and early on we had been 2-1 up thanks to goals from Jem and Will Hill. Steven Metheringham was in goal as Leadenham was absent and a couple of good saves from him kept us ahead. Both sides missed chances in the second half before Bridgford eventually proved too good for us.

The visit of Horncastle 2nds for our next league match was expected to give us a stern test. We fielded David Braunton and David Starr for the first time and Lloyd Morris-Fletcher was back for a one-off appearance and the game was over inside the first 20 minutes as we raced into a four-goal lead. It was our turn to enjoy dominance at the set piece and our short corners were too hot for Horncastle to handle. From our first, Clark picked up the pieces as a set play broke down to put us ahead, then Hollingworth nipped in to tuck home a second goal from another short corner.

Gray then got himself on the score sheet, then Horncastle briefly threatened a comeback but after Leadenham made a clearing save, Starr flicked the ball past the keeper after being left clear and having his initial shot well saved.

The rest of the half was a much more even affair, but we were keeping the ball well and moving it about sweetly, which meant that our visitors were feeding on scraps. Even when they did get through, Leadenham was in commanding form. The second half saw Horncastle enjoy more ball and they grabbed a goal from a short corner. Far from getting them back into the game, the goal gave us a bit of a kick up the behind and we surged forward once again.

We produced some excellent hockey and one of several sweeping moves was neatly swept home by Clark to put the gloss on a wonderful team performance. Starr's experience at a high level gave us a real touch of class on the right, and later on in the season up front, while Braunton was versatile enough to fit in anywhere and his driving runs down the right and sharp crossing would become a feature of our play throughout the season.

Frustration followed the weekend after as Long Sutton 4ths failed to show up, unable to raise a team. Captain Gray decided not to tell us and while the majority of us stayed on and enjoyed a club game and some training, there were one or two who were less than impressed and decided not to stick around. The 3-0 win awarded to us by default left us second – on goal difference – to Horncastle. Naturally, I claimed a hat-trick.

We were back in action down at Spalding where we took on their 4th team – a better outfit than their 5ths but the game proved no less of a challenge to us than the 6-3 win earlier in the season. Spalding started the stronger and along with my fellow defenders, I had to be on high alert and although we eventually settled and started to put some pressure on

Spalding, this week our short corners weren't working and opportunities were spurned.

Several other chances were missed until Paul Hollingworth finally took one to put us 1-0 up. We couldn't, despite further pressure, add a second and that allowed Spalding the opportunity to get back into the game. And it was one they took when from a short corner, Leadenham saved the initial shot but was powerless to prevent the follow-up being flicked past him from close range.

After half-time, what Spalding did next was to effectively park the bus and try to hold on for a draw or catch us on the break. This was something entirely new for us as we had been so used over the last few years of being on the receiving end of teams dominating possession and raining shots down on our goal. This was now a challenge that we had to face up to:

"The next goal in the game after half-time was likely to be decisive but it took a while to arrive as wave after wave of Grantham attacks were repelled by the massed ranks of Spalding defence, despite the best efforts of David Nix and David Braunton who worked well down the right to put Spalding under severe pressure. It was Clark who finally broke the deadlock after he received a pass from Willey, turned, beat his man and shot past the goalkeeper to register his fifth goal of the season."

With our passing game largely nullified by the Spalding defensive strategy, I urged Clark and Gray to instead try changing tack and dribble past two or three players to try and open up some space. As it happened, Willey's pass to create the goal was an absolute belter, splitting the defence through the tightest of gaps, allowing Clark the space he needed to score what was an important goal, not just in the game, but in the season overall. We had held our nerve, and broken through.

From there, we were never going to lose, especially as Spalding had to abandon their spoiling tactics and the game became more open. Hollingworth never stopped running all day and he grabbed his second goal to make it 3-1 and we finished the game strongly with a wonderful goal:

"Further Spalding attacks were cleared by Grantham's disciplined defence and they applied the coup de grace to a solid performance when they added a fourth goal with a devastating break at the end of the game. After Spalding won a short corner, Leadenham saved and the ball was cleared to Braunton, who found David Nix on the right wing. In an instant, the ball was transferred from one circle to the other where Gray was on hand to sweep home."

Now we had the chance to go back to the top of the table when Alford 2nds came to visit us at the Meres. We repeated our fast start that we had managed against Horncastle and within minutes Ben Willey – son of Andrew – had given us the lead when he was given the freedom of the shooting circle. Oli Phillips had a goal disallowed but we were guilty of sitting back and no doubt a touch of complacency crept into our game.

As we then struggled to clear our lines, Alford took advantage with a clever long ball game, bypassing the midfield to put our defence under pressure and eventually we succumbed and went into half-time with the scores level. Alford would have been the happier of the two sides as we had again dominated possession, territory and the short corner count, but couldn't make it pay.

After being asked to raise our game we immediately did so and Hollingworth restored our advantage soon after the break, nipping in front of his marker and sweep home at the near post, showing his strikers' instinct for goal. We continued to press and might have added further goals but for some solid defending from Alford and our own profligacy in front of goal, but boosted by our performance the week before, we stayed patient, and building the ball nicely from the back, we continued with our short passing game and it began to pay dividends.

"Man of the match Alex Clark combined well with captain Mark Gray, Starr and Phillips as Grantham took control of the crucial midfield battle and exerted themselves on the game, patiently building the ball from the back and surging into attack with some lovely short passing moves that had their opponents chasing shadows. Finally they moved into a more comfortable two-goal lead when an attack down the left offered Phillips the opportunity to cross the ball at pace and after his pass bounced back off a post, with the goalkeeper completely wrong-footed, Starr reacted well to knock the ball home."

Although Starr scored from about two yards out, it was a goal that might have been missed by others, as both he and the goalkeeper were initially wrong-footed as the ball changed direction after hitting the post. It wasn't a move straight from the training ground but such was Starr's coolness in front of goal that it looked mighty impressive. Starr might have then completed a hat-trick but his drag flicks were beaten away by the goalkeeper.

Our goalkeeper, Leadenham, had a quiet afternoon. No short corners were conceded and apart from picking the ball out of the goal, he hardly touched the ball as we went two points clear of Long Sutton with 18 points to 16.

We moved closer to the end of the winter programme with the trip to Cranwell that many of us had been looking forward with a mixture of anticipation, excitement and perhaps a little nervousness. We would be playing against old friends Simon Chambers and Ben Lane, but also knew full well that the game would not be easy as we looked to protect our place at the top of the table. And so it proved.

It was a tight game, with tackles flying in and neither side able to wrest control early, although we gradually forced into a strong position. Leadenham touched the ball just thrice in the first half and two Leadenham short corners came to nothing. By contrast, ours were in good working order again.

"Grantham's set pieces were dramatically improved from recent matches and their opening goal came from an early corner when Starr sent a drag flick spearing past former Grantham 'keeper Simon Chambers in the Leadenham goal."

Hollingworth had a goal disallowed soon after and we then pulled out a two-goal advantage, Clark keeping his composure to slip the ball past the onrushing Chambers which allowed Starr to sweep home. One of the reasons we knew we would be in for a challenge was because of Chambers. We had first-hand experience of how sharp a goalkeeper he was and to get two goals past him in short order was the sort of thing we had dreamt of. He then performed brilliantly to repel several chances from Starr, Hollingworth and Phillips to keep Leadenham in the game.

We continued to play solidly in the second half but were far less incisive and precise than we had been. David Nix was having one of his games where he pops up everywhere to set up attacks but our edge had gone, without ever threatening to concede. We didn't park the bus, but we certainly did enough to protect our lead and Leadenham were unable to come back.

"An outstanding team effort was epitomised by David Nix pulling off a reverse stick tackle inside his own circle and man-of-the-match Pennington enjoying a rare dribbling foray deep inside the Leadenham 25 and Starr was forced to fill in at centre back when Pennington was briefly forced from the field with a knee injury."

It wasn't the dreaded ligaments, just a bruise, thankfully. Andy Willey, who had umpired the match, challenged me afterwards as to why our performance had dropped off in the second half. I couldn't give a brilliant answer, but in all honesty, it was up to Leadenham to come out and play in the second half – not us. We did enough, and that was enough for me. Matters were also complicated by the low sun making it difficult for both umpires and players to get a full picture of the action in certain areas of the pitch.

A horrible spell of cold weather then hit the area in early December and when we got to Boston for our final league game of the year, we found the pitch borderline playable, such was the hardness of the frost. The sun came out and warmed things up a little but we were forced to start with 10 men and captain Gray was also absent.

We missed him although Clark and Phillips put in admirable shifts in the centre of the park but the experience of Boston's players ensured we all had our work cut out. Boston put together some good early moves and I had to clear a few dangerous crosses – one of them illegally bouncing off my knee – and Leadenham was also called into early action.

Our attacking play then earned us into good opportunities, Starr had a drag flick saved and sustained pressure from us got us into the lead as Starr finished off with his reverse stick again after a shot from Jem Hill had been saved.

Our problems continued early in the second half when Starr limped off with the calf injury that would all but his end his season. Boston used the one-man advantage cleverly to put us under pressure and for the rest of the afternoon, our defensive mettle would be tested to the limit. Boston had several short corners that were either saved or missed and when one was illegally stopped, they had a penalty stroke to equalise. There would have been little chance of us coming back had they scored it but Leadenham saved the day.

This was another hard-earned victory and an incredibly satisfying one. For more than half the match we had played with 10 men and lacking the experience of Starr and Gray, we produced a mature performance, particularly as a few Boston players appeared to be intent on winding us up. One player rammed his stick between my legs as I had the ball. I stopped, and was about to remonstrate with umpire Dean Newell when he did blow his whistle to award the foul, telling me he was waiting to see if I was going to play on. It would have been a touch difficult considering I would have had to effectively jump a small hurdle before doing so.

"Not with my knees," I told him.

That ended the winter, and we were again fortunate to not lose any matches to bad weather. The last thing we would have wanted later on in the season would have been a fixture pile-up. We were delighted to sit atop the league; it made a lovely Christmas present.

10. GLORIOUS FINALE – SPRING 2012

2012 started perfectly for us as we welcomed Spalding 5ths to the Meres. The game began after a poignant and impeccably well respected minute's silence was observed by both teams and onlookers in memory of Spalding goalkeeper Paul Howden, who had died in December.

Spalding, who play in maroon, had not turned up with a change of shirt so were forced to wear green bibs, which at times with the sun low in the sky, didn't make our task any easier. Mind, seeing as we came off the pitch having won 8-0, we had little to complain about.

Paul Hollingworth scored four of the goals, completing his hat-trick before half-time and the other goals came from David Braunton, David Nix, Oli Phillips and Andy Nix. Hollingworth had put us 2-0 up when I noticed that Nix on the wing was beating his man regularly but failing to cross the ball accurately. I suggested to captain Mark Gray that he switch Nix with Braunton, and the move worked almost instantly, Braunton beating a number of players and laying on Hollingworth's third strike.

Spalding's young front line gave us the odd nervy moment but no more than that and 3-0 at half-time left us in a position from which we would not be beaten. We played a high line in defence, denying them any space and ensuring that when they did break, we mopped up the ball and swiftly turned defence into attack.

"One such move resulted in their fourth goal - probably the best of the match as Braunton, (James) Kerr, (Andy) Nix, (Mark) Richardson and Phillips moved the ball from the right wing, round the back and then up the left wing, eventually laying the ball back to David Nix, who placed the ball perfectly into the corner of the goal across the goalkeeper."

Braunton then got on the score sheet, rewarded for persistence after initial shots were saved and Andy Nix converted a short corner as the goals kept coming. Spalding briefly threatened, earning a short corner that we were able to clear and we continued to batter Spalding's goal.

Hollingworth grabbed his fourth when he guided David Nix's shot into the goal and he then set up Phillips to crash home from the top of the circle. Unsurprisingly, Hollingworth was named as our man of the match.

We knew that the next match, the home fixture against Long Sutton, could be the most important of the season. Although they had games in hand so were a few points back, they had proved the stiffest challenge we had faced up to that point and we were expecting a similarly difficult match.

In the past, for whatever reason, we had struggled to perform on the days when it really mattered. I recall games against Atherstone and Kettering when had we been able to produce our best form, we would have gained results. Today was another day where we hoped we would do ourselves justice, knowing that a good result could set us up nicely for the rest of the season.

Benjie Groom had returned to the club and after a slight confusion over his transfer, was eventually cleared to play for us with this game marking his second 'debut'. He couldn't have made a better impression than smashing the ball into the top corner in the second minute. Admittedly, there was a deflection, but it looked mighty impressive and just reward for us making a sharp start to the game, both Groom and Hollingworth having early opportunities before we did get into the lead.

Ahead, we employed the high line; giving Long Sutton little room to play and we were able to latch on to any loose balls and simply start attacking once again. We were a team completely confident in one another, happy to pass the ball backwards, safe in the knowledge that it would soon be making its way forwards and our running off the ball caused Long Sutton all manner of problems.

We had enjoyed the lions' share of possession and territory but Long Sutton held out to keep the score at 1-0 at the break. We continued with more of the same after the break but the crucial second goal wouldn't come. Once we got one goal, we almost immediately added another to put the game beyond our opponents:

"A typically industrious run from Nix gave Groom space at the top of the circle and his reverse shot nestled into the bottom corner and less than 60 seconds later, Grantham had extended their lead further. Phillips, who had plenty of ball on the left wing, crept infield and after more outstanding work from man-of-the-match Groom, was picked out in space and he made no mistake."

We took our foot of the gas after that and Long Sutton had a few decent chances – including a short corner – and goalkeeper Will Leadenham didn't touch the ball all game. The win left us nine points clear and it was no longer Long Sutton who were our chief rivals – we would be battling with Horncastle and Leadenham from here on in.

We hadn't been a happy team following the 1-0 defeat away at Long Sutton but this was a pleasing result, and we were humbled to see the following in Long Sutton's own report that they posted online:

"Sutton came into the game more in the 2nd half and with a little more luck could have easily equalised, however the result was decided with the sucker punch of two quick goals for Grantham which gave them a 3-0 win. Sutton can take credit from an excellent performance (sic) against a team that could be playing a number of divisions higher..."

The bad weather kept us from playing at all in the next couple of weeks and we were back in action with the trip to take on Horncastle 2nds in our next fixture. It was a cold day, the pitch was slippery and neither side played with much fluency. If anything, they played the better hockey but we were resilient, at times desperate perhaps, and escaped with a 1-1 draw.

It meant our run of eight successive wins came to an end but we weren't too bothered about that. We started poorly and Horncastle would rue missing a couple of good early chances, Leadenham in action early for a change. We gradually found our feet and ground out some possession, although when we got in front of goal, we were either thwarted by Horncastle's defending or simply out of luck, until Clark tucked the ball home from a short corner.

The lead didn't last long as Horncastle broke on the left wing, outnumbering our defence and beating Leadenham from close range. Our luck deserted us in comical fashion soon after when David Nix's shot hit Hollingworth in the head instead of troubling the goalkeeper. Hollingworth bravely played on and continued to cause problems up front even though further goals eluded us.

If any team was more likely to score, it was the home side, but it took us defenders to clear, block and save a series of short corners to keep the scores level. Horncastle had a goal disallowed, the umpires eventually deciding that the ball hadn't travelled the required distance before being played into the circle. It was a reprieve, no doubt, and we came away relieved to have avoided defeat.

I struggled towards the end of the game as the dreaded knee pain had returned. I hoped it was just a reaction and nothing more serious and it didn't stop me making enough tackles and interceptions to be named as our man of the match. After this match, two more wins would in all likelihood earn us promotion; two wins and a draw from four matches would guarantee it.

Win number one came down at Long Sutton 4ths, who we outclassed to win 7-0. David Nix scored a hat-trick, avoiding our own players' heads this week. He opened the scoring within give minutes and Groom had added a second shortly after and although Long Sutton tried hard to get back into the game, we stood firm at the back. I say 'we', but I wasn't playing, feeling the need to rest my knee, which unfortunately, was giving me the same problems it had before it flared up seriously. At least this time I knew better then to try and run it off, even if it meant I might miss out on our promotion.

2-0 at half-time in Long Sutton was the signal for us to push forward and look for more goals but again it was Sutton who started the brighter, excellent defensive work from Andy Nix and Richardson being required to keep a clean sheet. David Nix added his second from a short corner to increase our lead and begin to kill the game off as a contest. Clark wrote afterwards:

"The fourth goal was a well-worked move on the right of midfield, culminating in Groom squaring the ball into the danger area for striker Paul Hollingworth to finish well from close range.

"By this stage, Grantham were in top gear and flying. Helped very much by excellent umpiring which aided the flow of the game, Gray and Clark were able to pick passes left, right and centre to create further opportunities for the remainder of the match.

"The only moment of danger for Grantham came as a speculative pass found its way through to a Long Sutton striker, but a tackle from Clark took the sting off the shot and allowed Ben Willey to clear the ball off the goal line, capping a good performance from him."

Braunton crashed home the fifth, Nix completed his hat-trick and the scoring was completed by Will Hill:

"The icing on the cake was added late in the game. A lovely breakaway one-two by Clark and Groom, put Clark through on goal, where he squared the ball unselfishly to Will Hill, being clattered by the 'keeper for his troubles, allowing Hill to finish comfortably at the back post for Grantham's seventh."

If other results went our way, it was possible that a win over Spalding 4ths at the Meres would seal the league title and promotion.

If there were any nerves around, they were quickly settled with an early goal. Sustained early pressure on the Spalding goal led to Oli Phillips being given time and space in the circle and he made no mistake.

"A second followed not long afterwards. Good interplay between forwards Benjie Groom and Dave Braunton on the right found Groom on the byline, where he delivered a telling ball to Hollingworth at the top of the circle, who finished accomplishedly, despite the 'keepers best efforts."

Spalding responded with a number of attacks on the Grantham goal but they were repelled and Phillips scored again to put us three goals clear. It had been a devastating half of hockey and we weren't finished yet. After excellent work from Gray had bamboozled the Spalding defence, Muzamill Pirwani pounced on a loose ball and made it 4-0, registering his first goal for the club. He had the ball in the goal again soon after but Phillips' pass into the circle had been dangerously lifted and it was correctly disallowed.

We were again possibly guilty of easing off in the second half and Spalding came into the game more and more, keeping the ball although never seriously threatening our goal, the experienced defensive line of Andy Nix, Graham Johnson and Nick Wraith doing a fine job.

Braunton scored after a short corner, Groom tucked one away and the goal that put the icing on the promotion-winning cake was scored by Phillips, who secured a hat-trick for good measure. Two years earlier, his twin brother Adam had scored the hat-trick that ended our 1,309-day long wait for a league win. This hat-trick ensured that we had gone from the bottom of a big pile to the top of a smaller one; and we had done it in style – with two games to spare.

During our time in the Midlands League, we had aimed to not concede 100 goals per season. In our first season in the East League, with two games to go, we had conceded just nine, and had realistic ambitions of keeping our goals against figures to single figures. While the goals came thick and fast, our defensive effort was also one to be proud of. 7-0 wins might be impressive but your season can be defined by grinding out results in tough games.

The clean sheets we kept against Boston (1-0), Leadenham (2-0) and Long Sutton (3-0) were the defining performances of the season for me. It might be stating the obvious, but by making ourselves very hard to score against, we had become a very hard team to beat. We also knew that eventually we would grab a goal ourselves, resisting the urge to panic if things didn't go our way.

There was no danger of that happening up at Alford, where we smashed our way to a 14-0 win. Clark opened his report as follows:

"After securing a fully-deserved league title last week, Grantham delivered a lethal display to dispatch a mid-table Alford side with consummate ease and keep up their devastating form, now with 28 unanswered goals in only 3 games.

"On a beautiful sunny day in Skegness, Grantham once again began a game by rattling through the gears, finding multitudes of space and creating openings from the offset. However, still at 0-0, when one of Grantham's attacks broke down, the home side counter-attacked downfield to create their only meaningful chance of the game, the Alford forward sweeping narrowly wide much to Grantham's relief.

"Needless to say, the momentary defensive lapse was not repeated as Grantham maintained disciplined concentration throughout and sweeper Mark Richardson had a commanding performance, stifling Alford completely, and the home side did not even get another shot the whole game."

It must have been one-way traffic in the extreme. 14 goals in 70 minutes equates to a goal every five minutes and it was the sort of thrashing that this time last year, we were being handed ourselves. And for 13 minutes of the game, we were down to 10 men, Groom sin-binned for his reaction to an Alford foul. He made amends in the second half by scoring four times in an overwhelming display of attacking hockey. There were a couple of unlikely goal scorers as Wraith grabbed a brace and Johnson, shifted to play up front for the second half, bagged his maiden goal with a reverse stick flick as we scored our 28th goal in three matches.

But could we beat Leadenham at home to complete the perfect record at The Meres?

We knew we would have to work hard and indeed conceded our tenth goal of the season shortly after we had taken the lead. With a number of us – your author included – missing through injury David Starr made an unlikely comeback from injury, scoring the opening goal only for Leadenham to equalise from a short corner.

Starr showed his class by putting us back ahead with a strike that flew into the top corner and then extended the lead by adroitly finishing off a sweeping move to put us 3-1 up. Ben Willey made it 4-1 after a goal-bound shot had been blocked illegally but Leadenham were not done with their scoring, a mazy run from their attacker culminating in a reverse stick shot that beat our Leadenham – goalkeeper Will.

> "Leadenham hit back when a mazy run from their centre forward culminated in a reverse stick shot that beat Will Leadenham but there was just time left in the game for Grantham to hit their fifth.

After another goalbound shot was saved illegally, a penalty flick was awarded and with the last stroke of the season, Starr powered the ball past former Grantham stopper Simon Chambers."

It was a fitting end to an enthralling game, and a fitting end to a season unlike any other I had endured or enjoyed with Grantham. In our 16 matches, we had won 14, drawn one and lost one, scoring 73 goals and conceding just 11, for a goal difference of +62. We were 10 points clear of our nearest challengers, who ended up as Leadenham, although for most of the second half of the season, they were engaged in a battle for second place.

When we moved across to the East League, I had it in my mind that by the 2013/14 season, we ought to be playing in Division 5, giving us two seasons to get promoted. We had exceeded my own expectations but had also done it by playing an exciting brand of hockey. The seasons of heartache slogging it out and getting thrashed in the Midlands had served us well in building our character and ensuring that we never took things for granted.

The likes of David Nix, Gray and James Kerr had been through, as I had, the full rollercoaster of emotions having played regularly for the first team longer than anybody who featured this season. There was no great celebration that I can remember, but then, just as had been the case when we ended the drought against Long Buckby, I hobbled off and left the players to it. I had played my part, but again, this was their moment. I would get my moment of glory a little later in the year.

2011/12 SEASON IN REVIEW

EAST LEAGUE DIVISION 6 NORTH WEST (NORTH)

Opponents	Home	Away
Alford 2nds	Won 3-1	Won 14-0
Boston 2nds	Won 4-1	Won 1-0
Horncastle 2nds	Won 5-1	Drew 1-1
Leadenham	Won 5-2	Won 2-0
Long Sutton 3rds	Won 3-0	Lost 1-0
Long Sutton 4ths	Won 3-0	Won 7-0
Spalding 4ths	Won 7-0	Won 4-1
Spalding 5ths	Won 8-0	Won 6-3

League Table

Grantham 43 points, Leadenham 33, Long Sutton 3rds 31, Horncastle 29, Boston 24, Spalding 4ths 23, Alford 18, Spalding 5ths 9, Long Sutton 4ths 3

Grantham earned promotion to East League Division 5 NW

1,309 DAYS LATER

11. HONOURED AT LAST – SUMMER 2012

At the 2011 annual club awards ceremony, I had given a slightly rambling speech – in my then capacity of chairman – about how it had been a difficult season and that Andy Willey and myself had spent more time on the phone to each other than we had our respective partners. That was an unwise joke to try to make seeing as I was single at the time. The atmosphere was so different 12 months on with both men and women – who had finished 11th in the Lincolnshire league despite on several occasions struggling to raise a full side – in good spirits.

We had an excellent evening and I was delighted to win not one, but two awards. First, Ben Willey was named as the men's Young Player Of The Year for his efforts in various positions during the season and after Clark was given the Captain's Player Of The Year, it was my turn to go up and accept the Players' Player Of The Year trophy. Clark thoroughly deserved his award and he must have come close to sweeping both, such was his outstanding performance throughout the league campaign. He will be missed as heads off around the world and then to university.

Incoming captain Oli Phillips then took the floor to hand out even more awards and I was up again to receive the Defender Of The Year award. On a tight budget, he had stuck a printed out copy of a Land Rover Defender onto a paper plate. There was the obligatory 'booby' prize for Gray and everybody was highly amused. At least he didn't have to deal with the dirty pints that I had to at university, although Phillips might still be paying for it now had he gone down that route on the night.

A few weeks later, I received a phone call from chairman David Sykes.

"John, I wonder if you'd be available in a couple of weeks to go down to Letchworth and pick up the league trophy?" he asked.

"How far down your list am I?"

"Quite far."

It turned out that if you didn't send somebody along to pick up the trophy, a fine of £100 would be levied so it would be cheaper for us to send someone down and make a contribution to their petrol costs. I agreed to go as I knew it would be a nice way to finish off the season.

It was a wonderfully hot day – perhaps not the best driving conditions – but no one was complaining, given how bad the start of the 2012 summer was. I was the first person at the venue; Grantham were winning things on and off the pitch. I believe I speak for perhaps 95% of those present at the day that we sat through the meeting beforehand, mainly awaiting our chance to get our hands on the trophies we had won and a free lunch.

The formalities over, the trophy handing out began and before too long it is my turn. I didn't really have to do too much. I wandered up, picked up the trophy and a framed printout of the league standings and thanked the league officials several times as I smiled for the cameras that weren't being readied for me. Nobody else had been available to come down with me for just such a purpose.

Never mind, we had the trophy and as I write it sits proudly by my television, flanked by the framed league table and my Player Of The Year award. The Defender Of The Year plate sits behind me, propped up by a phone and in between some family photos.

So what now? Already, plans have begun for the 2012/13 season. Phillips has got seriously organised on Facebook and has already picked a provisional team to play against Wisbech on 15th September. I am in it, although I am still concerned about where my knee is. A couple of pre-season mixed tournaments and then some friendlies will confirm exactly what sort of shape I am in.

There is a quiet confidence about the club and although our first aim has to be to survive relegation, there is a feeling that we should be able to hold our own against better opposition. It is interesting when looking at the line-up of the league to see that we only play two other first teams – Boston and Louth. The rest are a mix of 2nds, 3rds and 4ths. That is exactly why we made the move to the East League and we are delighted to be finding our level, and enjoying our hockey again.

If the 2012/13 season is half as good as this one, then I can't wait for this time next year.

1,309 DAYS LATER

EPILOGUE – JOURNEY'S END?

I started by mentioning that this has been quite a journey. From a personal point of view, from Minehead to Grantham via Coventry and Taunton, it's been an interesting and colourful one, to say the least. As a club, Grantham has evolved greatly over the years, and we have gone from whipping boys in the Midlands to a team on the up in the East.

Our journey could still be just beginning. As we continue to build for the future, who knows whether our success might just inspire a few local youngsters to pick up a stick? If the Great Britain teams can perform well at their home Olympic Games, perhaps local youngsters will be similarly inspired? I was fortunate enough to meet up with the British hockey Olympians a few weeks prior to the games, interviewing, amongst others, Crista Cullen and Richard Mantell.

I thought it an apt moment to mention to Richard how in my youth I had played against his brother Simon – unfortunately injured and therefore not selected. My story-telling didn't quite have the effect I was looking for.

"Richard, it's a pleasure to meet you. Many years ago, I played against your brother when he was at Millfield," I said, struggling to make my voice heard over a busy evening's entertainment.
"Oh, what was his name?" he replied.
I was a little confused, unaware that he had misheard me completely. "Er, Simon," I added.
The confusion now became apparent when he asked me, "Does your brother still play?"
I broke into a smile and thought some sign language might now help my cause. "No, no, sorry," I said, pointing to myself as I did so.

"I played against *your* brother Simon."

We were both rescued from this bizarre exchange by the red light on the camera alerting me to the fact it was time to ask some proper questions, and he spoke superbly about what it might be like to play in front of a home crowd in London and what good shape the team was in.

We might never play in front of a crowd of thousands, and we will probably not be giving interviews at high-profile events in the capital, but his words could so easily apply to Oli Phillips as he looks ahead in confident mood to what is ahead for Grantham Hockey Club. When you wait 1,309 days for a league victory, you feel like you've seen it all. When you've had snatched so many defeats from the jaws of victory, you know not to get complacent when things are going your way. When you've seen players seriously injured in front of you and suffered injury yourself, you make sure you enjoy the times when you come off the pitch feeling strong and healthy.

I am glad that we got extensive local newspaper coverage following our landmark win and I hope that we did make the nationals as well. I hope that this story might inspire people or teams in a similar predicament. Sport is cyclic – no team can remain at the top indefinitely, and similarly, no team can remain at the bottom forever. It is simply a matter of time, of self-belief and of making brave decisions when necessary. The good times will come.

However, at the end of the day, it is great to win, but that isn't what it is all about. We turn out at the weekend – and sometimes for training – because we enjoy the sport, and we enjoy meeting up with people who we wouldn't have known without the game. As a bonus, we have formed strong relationships, lost, drawn and then won together through a period of time in which many things in the world – and our small part of it – have changed. We are still 11 men representing Grantham trying to do our best. We will still enjoy a drink with our opponents afterwards, no matter what the score. We will still be frustrated by silly little things like litter on the pitch, goals not being put out on time, players turning up late and coming up with spurious excuses as to why they cannot attend a training session. Yet, once we cross that white line, all is forgotten, we pull together and work as a team. Like a family. The hockey family.

It is, after all, not so much about the destination, but the journey that is important. Thanks for jumping on board.

1,309 DAYS LATER

APPENDIX

Press release sent out to the world following 10th October 2010 win over Long Buckby:

1,309 Reasons To Be Cheerful

Grantham Hockey Club's Men's 1st team yesterday (Saturday 10th October) ended a run of more than three years without a league victory when they beat Long Buckby 5-1 to open their account for the season in the Bodykraft League East Midlands Division Two.

Their last league win came on 11th March 2006, 1,309 days before Saturday, when they beat Loughborough Sharks by three goals to two, also at home, but the wait was finally ended by a largely dominant performance over league newcomers Long Buckby, who were downed by a hat-trick from Adam Phillips and a goal apiece from long-serving captain Simon Higgs and youngster Christian Keogh.

Having gone through the entire 2006/7, 2007/8 and 2008/9 seasons without a single win, shipping 382 goals in the process, the win comes as a huge relief for the club, which has recently lost the services of a number of players; some leaving for university, some moving to other clubs.

"In my short time at the club, I have seen a number of talented young players leave for university just when they become accomplished players," chairman John Pennington, who missed out on playing due to a knee injury, commented.

"That means we rely heavily on younger players who are effectively learning league hockey in a first-team environment, which is tough, but it is a great credit to them that they have worked hard and played a key role in today's win.

"I am very proud that for the first time since I joined the club in late 2007, I am able to report a league victory for the men's first team and I am extremely confident that I won't be waiting another 1,309 days - which would be sometime in April 2013 - to talk about a win again."

15-year-old winger Alex Clark, who only made his first-team debut last week in a 5-0 loss to Kettering, put the three-year wait into perspective: "All I know is that 11th March 2006 was about six months before I started playing hockey," he commented.

Fellow 15-year-old Patrick Cutmore was also making his league debut for the club after joining in the close season from Beeston while fellow new recruit Benjie Groom played his part and managed to take a win in just his second league appearance.

Captain Simon Higgs was one of two players (along with centre-forward David Nix) involved in the match who had played in 2006, and he said: "I'm very pleased with the win, it was a strong performance from a a new group of players that is still in the process of gelling as a unit.

"Having played back in 2006 when we won three times that season, I certainly didn't expect us to be waiting so long for another win, although we have beaten teams in friendlies and tournaments in the meantime. I certainly hope that I won't be waiting another three years for another league win."

Pennington added: "While I was disappointed not to be on the pitch, that was tempered by the shared feeling of joy around the group. Having had a three-year break from the game before moving to Grantham, I haven't dared to work out when the last league victory I played a part in was.

"Hopefully the nucleus of this side will bring us more victories in the years to come."

The 13 men who played in yesterday's win were: Simon Chambers, Simon Higgs (captain)*, Andy Barton, Adam Phillips, Ben Lane, James Kerr, Christian Keogh, Hayden Richards, Benjie Groom, Patrick Cutmore, Alex Clark, Henry Young, David Nix*.

* played on 11th March 2006 against Loughborough Sharks.

1,309 DAYS LATER

ABOUT THE AUTHOR

Defender John Pennington first played for Grantham in 2007, was club chairman between 2009 and 2011 and has been on the club's committee since 2008. An experienced sports journalist, this is his third book.

He has lived and worked in England and France, began his hockey career at Minehead and West Somerset Hockey Club and graduated from University of Warwick in 2006.

He has written two books on cricket, one a retrospective on England's 2009 Ashes success and the other a (brief) diary of his own attempt to play a season of club cricket in Lincolnshire.

http://www.jspennington.com / Twitter @jspennington